Patton's Complete Guide to Productivity Improvement

Patton's Complete Guide to Productivity Improvement

John A. Patton

ama com A Division of
American Management Associations

I would like to dedicate this book to my wife, Helen, for her patience, tolerance, and total support in all my endeavors.

Library of Congress Cataloging in Publication Data

Patton, John A.
  Patton's Complete guide to productivity improvement.

  Includes index.
  1. Industrial productivity. I. Title.
II. Title: Complete guide to productivity
improvement.
HD56.P36   658.3'14   81-69374
ISBN 0-8144-5697-9   AACR2

© 1982 AMACOM
A division of American Management Associations,
New York.
All rights reserved. Printed in the United States of
America.

Third Printing

Preface

During the 30 years I have worked in the management consulting field and served as an executive in one of our nation's largest corporations, one basic observation has continually occupied my mind. This is the undeniable fact that most industrial leaders already *know* what their problems are. I'll go one step further and state that many managements and the consultants they retain also know the answers to many of these problems. The common ailment in today's management community centers on a lack of will—plain, ordinary apathy—when it comes to implementing what is frequently an obvious solution to many of their serious problems.

I would like to feel that this book will provide the necessary tools to enable managers not only to recognize their problems, but also to resolve their difficulties by implementing the required solutions. I sincerely believe that only in this manner can America achieve the productivity improvement that is so badly needed if we are to survive as a major industrial power in the years ahead.

Let me say that if you are only mildly disturbed by the things you are about to read, I will be disappointed. Frankly, I hope to get you so worked up that you will go back to your company and do something about the productivity gap, which, if left unchecked, could well turn the long-cherished American dream into a terrifying nightmare.

John A. Patton

Acknowledgments

To list all the clients, friends, and business associates whose thoughts and services over the past 30 years have contributed directly or indirectly to this volume would probably fill another book.

I am personally very proud of the contents of this book. It is the result of my lifelong experience in productivity improvement and cost reduction. Despite this, I am aware of my own shortcomings, one of which is that I have never been accused of being a master of the English language. The reason I emphasize this point is that the book could have never been written without the organization, rewriting, and finesse brought to it by *Jack Lewis,* my associate for the past 12 years.

I am further indebted to *Robert Kelly,* whose research of our industrial scene was most helpful. In addition, I owe a deep vote of gratitude to *Gerald Dunbar,* who contributed liberally to the finished product. Special appreciation is also offered to *Perry Pascarella* and *William Schleicher,* who provided valuable critiques, and to *Dr. John Enell,* who has given me good counseling and advice over many years. Last, but not least, my sincere thanks to *Edmund Cyrol,* a capable consultant, who reviewed portions of the text with an impartial eye and had the grace to tell me what was right and the courage to tell me where modifications were required.

Contents

Introduction

In every age, in every era, there are those who are not content to settle for occupational mediocrity. In America it began with the men and women who arrived on the tall-masted sailing ships in search of a better way of life in a strange and foreign land.

The optimism of some of these early-day settlers was later diminished by conditions in the crowded cities. Many of these pressed westward across the dusty plains and High Sierra in a valiant attempt to tap the seemingly inexhaustable resources of a vast, unexplored nation. They came, they settled, and by their own sweat and determination they built a huge network of farms and markets and railroads. They worked in our nation's factories and mines and steel mills. Their success at these endeavors was respected and emulated by succeeding generations.

Their knowledge of economic principles was, by the most charitable definition, marginal. Despite this they were aware of the basic fact that to secure a day's wages it was first necessary to contribute a day's work.

Looking at the situation in retrospect one might argue that this early-day philosophy may have been based more on the principles of survival than on deprivation and dedication to hard work. These primitive people, you see, had not yet discovered that it was possible to survive by a superficial work effort, or to allot themselves benefits from public funds.

They may have had some difficulty putting their thinking into words, but there was a general feeling in those days that people should feel responsibility toward their government rather than expecting benefits and entitlements from it.

During the 1920s a few financiers were diverted momentarily from the rising Dow Jones averages by an article in *The Wall Street Journal* that reported the situation in Germany, where it took a wheelbarrow full of money to buy a bag of groceries and workers had to be paid twice a day to keep up with the exploding rate of inflation. Shortly afterward the German mark predictably collapsed and the economic thinkers of the era shook their heads and clucked their tongues.

"How lucky we are to be living in a country where the national wealth is based on tangible assets," they said. "That could never happen in America. Our government is too trustworthy to print money without adequate backing. The American people are too responsible to allow themselves to be wiped out by a system based on government paternalism and flat currency."

It was during this period that industrial leaders first began to accept the premise that by producing more, everyone, including employees, could enjoy a better lifestyle. An example of this was the Model T Ford assembly line, after which Henry Ford announced that henceforth Ford Motor Company employees would be paid the hitherto unheard-of wage of five dollars a day. This is not to suggest that businessmen of an earlier era were not well aware that their employees' work effort had to be in excess of the income derived from the goods and services they produced. Otherwise they would have been out of business very soon. However, the term "productivity" as we regard it today was an abstract factor that was difficult to measure on an organizational basis and impossible to determine on a national scale.

A more formal interest in the subject of productivity began to surface when America became engulfed in one of the long series of crises that have marked our turbulent, and sometimes violent, history. In October 1929, stock prices, which had been rising dramatically since the close of World War I, plunged sharply. By the end of the year $15 billion had been wiped out. By 1931 that figure had risen to $50 billion.

Economic solvency for those companies that wished to survive the Great Depression was suddenly contingent upon the establishment of vigilant, and sometimes rigid, standards of productivity. Enforcement of these standards was, in view of the circumstances, relatively easy to accomplish. A worker either met the existing standards or was summarily relegated to the armies of men and women who occupied our nation's breadlines. And given an option of this type, individual productivity predictably remained high.

Even during the bleak years of World War II, productivity continued to grow at an acceptable rate. Much of this could be ascribed to an intense spirit of patriotism. And after the unpleasantness was over, the technology that had been spawned from the need to make better tanks and ships and aircraft was reconstructed to meet the demand for products that were denied for so long to a nation at war.

From a standpoint of long-range statistics, between 1889 and a period shortly after World War II the United States record for productivity growth had been outstanding. During this period individual output per worker had increased by a staggering 500%. And there was even more to come.

Based to a large degree on the impetus generated by desire for a better way of life, and aided by huge strides in technology, productivity continued to escalate for the next few decades. From 1947 to 1972 the productivity rate in this country rose by an average of 3.1% per year. By the end of the 1960s, however, a few danger signs began to surface.

In 1969 and 1970 our productivity gains fell to less than 1% a year, the most serious drop in 16 years. Another cyclical slowdown appeared in 1973, when productivity rose less rapidly than it had in 1971 and 1972.

The most alarming thing about these figures was the fact that during this same period our foreign trade partners were registering huge gains. Between 1965 and 1972 Japan chalked up an astounding 12% annual increase. Common Market countries during the same period showed productivity gains that ran about 6%. Even more alarming from a standpoint of national interest was the sobering statistic that among the 11 leading industrial nations in the non-Communist world, America ranked at the bottom in terms of productivity improvement.

During the first half of the 1960s, prices were fairly stable largely because output per employee hour gained at a rate of 3.6%, which was about the same rate of increase as hourly pay. Yet during the past decade, hourly pay has increased 7.8% while worker output increased only 1.6%. Compounded over a decade, a 6% inflation rate reduces purchasing power of fixed incomes by almost half.

This trend, unfortunately, shows no signs of improvement. The end result is continued inflation, rising taxation, a lowering of our standard of living, and the very real danger that the affluent society we have come to take for granted may be rapidly slipping away.

The seriousness of the situation demands that we ask ourselves, "What caused this sharp reversal in our productivity rate?" And it is here that the fingerpointing and buckpassing begin to manifest themselves.

The government with its infinite layers of bureaucracy has attempted to regulate industry until it has virtually emasculated all the former prerogatives of free enterprise. The unions seemingly demand more and more money for less and less work. Profits fall as costs rise. Meanwhile, management all too often sits back and wrings its hands for a decent interval and finally passes down the increased cost of operation to the consumer. This is accompanied by arguing, bickering, cajoling, and threatening. Dire consequences are predicted, yet virtually nothing constructive is done.

Whom do we blame for this appalling situation? And even more important, what, if anything, can be done about our nation's deteriorating rate of productivity, which, if left unchecked, could literally abolish the long-cherished American lifestyle?

Can we blame all our economic woes on the government? Or on organized labor? Or is it just possible that management can do much toward alleviating the situation by attempting to tidy up the dusty corners of its own house?

Judging by the thirty years I have worked in the management consulting field, a large portion of which was spent as president of my own company, I expect I must technically be labeled a manager. Yet the scope of my daily activities, for obvious reasons, often overlapped into the areas of both government and labor.

I have often felt like the kibitzer at a card game who was privileged to witness the mistakes made by everyone else simply by being at a neutral vantage point where I could observe the total scene. This book will consist of my observations during this period, plus an account of many of the problems faced by my clients and the various methods that have been successfully used to alleviate these difficulties.

one

The Productivity Crisis

America's diminishing rate of productivity is a sinister force that causes inflation, suppresses initiative, reduces living standards, increases taxes, creates unemployment, stifles innovation, and has been largely responsible for the most all-encompassing bureaucracy that has ever existed in the history of the world.

The productivity crisis that exists in America today was created by a multitude of factors, many of which are capable of masking themselves in an intense spirit of legitimacy. Yet collectively, like the individual components of a fission bomb, they represent a devastating potential force that could eventually obliterate the society we have built up so carefully over the centuries.

If these statements sound like an overreaction, it might be well to consider that most of the advantages we now enjoy were brought about by a continual escalation in the rate of employee productivity—by working smarter, not harder. This, in turn, enabled workers to earn more and to purchase more, and thus to acquire a better standard of living. Our modern homes, our automobiles, and all the countless niceties that are standard equipment in the average American family unit are solid testimony that this formula has been enormously successful. Otherwise, as unthinkable as it appears, the typical American family complex might well consist of a mule, a plow, and a log cabin with outdoor plumbing.

Our present lifestyle, if it could be observed by our forebears, would surely be viewed as a vision that could only be conjured up by something akin to Aladdin's magic lamp. And since this miracle was wrought by a simple device called "increased productivity," it might even be appropriate to draw an analogy between the two. Unfortunately, in recent years the flame in the magic lamp that has created these miracles has been flickering precariously, and, if present trends continue, might even be snuffed out forever.

Historically, productivity in the United States has shown an annual average increase of about 3.2%. Since 1967, however, the rate has dropped to approximately half that figure.* Viewed as a single statistical item, a productivity drop of 1.6% may not evoke too many sleepless nights for the average taxpayer, even though the figure represents a 50% decrease. However, to realize the full impact it is necessary to correlate this statistic with additional data. And when this is done the economic shape of things to come becomes very bleak indeed.

During the 1960s when productivity output per employee showed an annual gain of 3.6%, hourly pay increased at about the same rate. Accordingly, with the system in balance, the economy remained relatively stable. However, during the 1970s, hourly pay rose sharply while productivity improvement was cut in half. The end result has been rising prices, double-digit inflation, and a steadily diminishing standard of living for the vast majority of our nation's wage earners and a sizable portion of the business community. To even further intensify the problem, manufacturers of foreign goods, chiefly from Japan and West Germany, have somehow managed to achieve annual productivity gains of between 6% and 12%.* They are thus able to underprice American-made products with the inevitable result of reduced gross sales for American products, increased unemployment among American workers, higher unemployment

*"Recent Productivity Trends in the United States." Unpublished report by National Association of Manufacturers, Washington, D.C., 1978.

*Ibid.

benefits, and increased taxation to pay for these benefits in an economy that is already reeling from the effects of double-digit inflation.

The scope of this two-pronged assault on our industrial community can best be illustrated by citing a few historical facts.

The Impact of Foreign Imports

In 1978 the United States had a $35 billion trade deficit, with numerous markets being gobbled up by foreign competitors.* In one of our most basic industries, steel production, U.S. technological leadership and productivity have badly eroded. The Japanese have done so well in the business of exporting steel to America that federal intervention has become necessary. In 1977, imported steel, mostly from Japan, hit a record of 19.3 million tons. This was more than 20% of the total United States market for steel. Much of this steel was sold at prices below the United States market, and yet during this same period the Youngstown Sheet & Tube Company laid off 5,000 workers. Other American steel companies cut prices in order to compete, but they took huge losses. Ironically enough, not all the American steel industry's problems were generated by our admitted shortcomings in productivity or by cheap foreign labor. European steel producers readily concede that they have sold their steel below the cost of producing it simply to reduce unemployment. Put another way, the government subsidizes the mills in the belief that this is more politically desirable and less expensive than massive unemployment.

The unfair trade advantage is not confined to our European trade partners. According to a report in the October 30, 1978, issue of *Business Week,* Brazil drops taxes for its exporting companies. The Japanese government works

*H.L. Weisberg, "Export Control Export Expansion—Ways to Balance Our Balance of Trade." United States Chamber of Commerce, National Chambers Publications Fulfillment Department, Washington, D.C., 1979.

hand in glove with its industries, subsidizing them and helping them in every way possible to win superiority over foreign markets. Paradoxically, however, Japan has instituted numerous nontariff barriers that restrict foreign imports into *their* country, a practice that keeps its own economy strong and transfers its unemployment problems to the United States. Unfortunately, the problem faced by the steel industry is only one facet of the balance of trade crisis.

The International Trade Commission reports that foreign imports in the footwear industry hold almost 50% of the United States market. The number of workers in the United States shoe industry dropped 30% over a ten-year period, while the number of shoe manufacturers declined from 600 to 378.

The problems faced by Chrysler Corporation and the automotive industry in general, which have been generated primarily by the influx of foreign imports, are so critical that 300,000 auto workers are now unemployed. It has been reported in the Chicago *Tribune,* based on data supplied by Armco Steel Corporation, that each lost job costs state and federal governments $13,249. This figure consists of unemployment compensation paid to idled workers, plus trade adjustment allowances and the taxes that are lost to the government.

Some American manufacturers have turned to Mexico for cheap labor. Numerous American-owned plants are now operating south of the border and providing the Mexican economy with jobs. These are not wildcat operations. They include such well-known company names as RCA, Zenith, General Instruments, AMF, and American Hospital Supply Corporation.

The jobs that are lost through our foreign trade imbalance and reduced productivity are important, but the skills that go with them are equally important. In the event of a national emergency, the United States would find itself woefully lacking in the ability to produce many vitally needed products. We are becoming increasingly vulnerable.

The most obvious solution to the balance-of-trade crisis would appear to be trade barriers, tariffs, and embargoes.

But the United States is also an exporting nation, and these measures bring about retaliatory action. Moreover, tariffs applied to United States imports increase prices to United States consumers.

The Rise and Fall of American Innovation

According to historians, a bill was brought up during the nineteenth century requesting the United States Congress to close down the patent office because everything that could possibly be invented had already been patented. To the credit of politicians of that era, the bill was defeated and innovation went on to develop assorted gadgets like television, computers, guided missiles, the gasoline engine, and sliced bread. In fact, during the first half of the twentieth century, America led the world in innovation and inventive capacity. In the 1950s the United States was responsible for 82% of worldwide innovations. By the 1960s, according to a study made by the National Center for Productivity and Quality of Working Life, that figure had decreased to 55%. In addition to this, a later study conducted by the National Science Foundation about the issuance of new patents brought our innovative shortcomings even more sharply into focus. According to this study:

> During 1963 Americans were issued 66,715 patents.
> During 1963 foreign nationals were issued 274,947 patents.
> During 1973 Americans were issued 66,935 patents.
> During 1973 foreign nationals were issued 360,353 patents.

This indicates an increase of only .3% in American inventive capacity, even though the population increased 11% during the decade over which the data was computed. During the same period, however, foreign national patents increased 31%.

It's one of the economic facts of life that innovation and

productivity go hand in hand, and sad to state, the United States now appears to be seriously lacking in both areas. In an earlier era, individual initiative and willingness to take risks were rewarded. This was the basic ingredient that spawned a period of rapid innovation in the making of America. Men like Henry Ford, Bill Boeing, and George Westinghouse showed the entire world how huge new industries could be developed from their ideas. Today the spirit of innovation is being replaced by a new attitude of "Don't rock the boat while the ship is sinking." We are becoming a nation controlled by fear—fear of taking risks, fear of change, and fear of being sued. The United States sorely needs new business ventures. A U.S. Department of Commerce study conducted over a six-year period showed that *new* technical enterprises realized an average sales growth of 42.5% and employment growth of 41%. During the same period, existing businesses grew only 11.4% in sales and less than 1% in employment.

The economic stagnation over the past decade has steered the United States economy into a vicious cycle. Decreasing innovation and productivity result in fewer dollars being generated. This in turn allows fewer dollars for reinvestment in research and development and modernized equipment, forcing business to operate with obsolete machines, which generates fewer dollars, et cetera, et cetera, et cetera.

Additional research and development is desperately needed in the United States. During the past decade R&D expenditures have fallen sharply in this country. Meanwhile, other countries, especially the USSR, have been increasing R&D expenditures. Approximately half of all United States R&D expenditures are for defense. However, in Japan and West Germany, virtually all R&D expenditures are for promotion of economic development.* Being the military watchdog of the world is putting America at a monstrous disadvan-

*"Recent Productivity Trends in the United States." Unpublished report by National Association of Manufacturers, Washington, D.C., 1978.

tage from a standpoint of economics. The irony of the situation is that United States business and industry (the very people who are being hurt by this policy) are footing the bill. Perhaps we've allowed our national priorities to become mixed up.

The Three-Legged Stool

For over half a century, government, labor, and management have been engaged in a vast three-sided tug of war. The most curious thing about this engagement is that all three entities are vitally dependent upon one another and should instead be working toward common goals. I like to refer to this interdependency as a three-legged stool. If properly constructed and maintained, a three-legged stool can, as we know, take some pretty rough usage and still find solid footing. The problem with the stool representing government, labor, and management is that the glue that holds the stool together has deteriorated and all three legs have become loose and wobbly.

Let's examine some of the things that are presently being done to inhibit productivity gains by the three legs of this stool. Let's focus first on government.

Government

In a Universal Press syndicated column published September 10, 1981, James Kilpatrick pointed out that federal, state, and local governments employ nearly 18 million people. This adds up to about one out of every six people in the total workforce. The managers of these employees have little incentive to increase productivity. Why should they? In most cases the status and grade of government managers are based on the size of the budget and the number of staff workers under them rather than on individual performance. I defy anyone to design a more counterproductive system.

The proliferation of government jobs is easy to understand. The benefits far exceed those paid to workers in private industry. To name a few; retirement pay begins at age 55, with adjustments made for inflation after retirement. Fringe benefits typically exceed those offered by private business by 53%. A 1977 study determined that the federal government spent $7,174 on fringe benefits for each employee. During the same period, private companies averaged $4,677. With benefits and salary combined, the United States government spent an average of $21,110 for each federal employee. Private business spent $15,769. A recent study conducted by *U.S. News & World Report* (published in the November 13, 1978, issue) estimates that a federal worker retiring with a pension of $20,000 a year may have an $80,000 annuity after 20 years of retirement. Employees retiring from the private business sector on a $20,000-a-year pension generally receive no inflation adjustment in the years ahead.

In addition to paying superior wages, salaries, and pensions for work performed, government agencies are notorious for lack of productivity, unperceptiveness, ineffective work practices, and general inefficiency.

Paradoxically, government agencies produce virtually nothing to contribute to the economy. All they do is redistribute the wealth produced by private enterprise, thus effectively channeling it away from productive sectors into nonproductive ventures. Frequently government agencies spend more than is needed to justify their own existence. It is, in effect, the "in" thing to spend more money. Examples of our government's ineptitude would probably fill a hundred volumes of the size you hold in your hand. However, for the benefit of readers who may have been on Mars for the past half century, let me cite a few.

It costs one-third less to ship and insure a ten-pound parcel from my home in Phoenix, Arizona, to Washington, D.C., by private carrier than it does by United States Parcel Post. Furthermore, I can expect two to three days' faster service by the private carrier.

I can make a three-minute long-distance telephone call for less than I could 25 years ago. In this same period the cost of mailing a letter has gone up 450%. Incredibly, the United States attorneys were investigating AT&T for restraint of trade. It would make more sense if they asked AT&T to run the Post Office Department.

In the summer of 1980, the *Arizona Republic* published an article about the inspector general at the Department of Energy. This employee, after 28 years' government service, had uncovered various irregularities in his department, including:

- 42 long-distance phone calls made by a department employee to a "Dial-a-Dirty-Joke" number in St. Louis.
- Mixups in the department's gas mileage guide that allegedly cost $500,000.
- Loss of more than 100,000 pieces of internal mail in a one-year period.
- A possible $10 million shortage in oil delivered to a storage facility in Louisiana.
- Evidence that consulting firms hired by the DOE were paid salaries of $320 a day for their own consultants, considerably in excess of departmental guidelines.

When this employee turned over his findings to DOE secretary Charles W. Duncan instead of to his immediate boss the chief financial officer, his boss objected on the grounds that the report had not been submitted through proper channels. He later attempted to transfer the employee to Paris, France, as a form of punishment. The employee resisted on the grounds that he couldn't be expected to submit adverse findings through the very people he was expected to audit and, furthermore, shouldn't be banished from his own country simply for doing his job. The problem of whether or not to revise the organizational chain of command in the DOE or to retain the procedure of having the fox guard the chicken coop has now been submitted to the halls of Congress.

The High Cost of Government Regulation

Countless billions of dollars are spent each year by private enterprise simply to meet government regulations. These are dollars that could have been spent to improve productivity, advance technology, and create new jobs.

In their efforts to "protect" the United States citizens, legislators who sponsor programs designed to regulate business are smothering innovation, dramatically increasing the cost of products and services being offered to the public, and simultaneously increasing taxes to support the huge bureaucracy of the agencies that generate these rules and regulations. The bureaucrats are therefore robbing Americans not only of their money but of their basic freedom.

According to an article by A. N. Wecksler in the February 1979 issue of *Appliance Manufacturer*, the cost of filling out government forms needed to comply with all regulations is estimated at $107 billion. There are some 4,400 different government forms that have to be filled out by private business.

The article, titled "The High Cost of Government Regulation," goes on to state that government regulations increase the cost of a new home by $2,500 and the price of a new car by $666. Because of regulation you pay $42.50 more for a refrigerator, $26.90 more for a dishwasher, $191.00 more for a central air conditioner, $32.00 more for a gas furnace, $11.70 more for a vacuum cleaner, and $48.70 more for a color television. It often appears as if government agencies are more interested in penalizing businesses than in helping them improve safety and health standards.

In Dow Chemical Company alone, complying with federal regulations cost $186 million in a single year.* During this same period the government was complaining of a paper shortage! The high cost of paperwork alone is squeezing out thousands of small businesses, as well as potential new enterprises that simply can't afford the high cost of product liabil-

*Harrison Schmitt, "Engineering Is Underrepresented on Capitol Hill." *Professional Engineer,* August 1978.

ity insurance, preparation of government reports, and need-less regulations. Those that can are required to pass the additional cost of doing business down to consumers, thereby increasing inflation and reducing company produc-tivity.

The costs of operating the Department of Energy is many billion dollars a year, and it is staffed by as many em-ployees as one of our giant oil companies. Yet this monstrous bureaucracy produces no energy. OSHA has issued over 4,000 new regulations since 1971. Many of these have been ambiguous and confusing even to OSHA administrators.

The most aggravating thing about situations like those described above is that attempting to get changes in estab-lished regulations is usually an exercise in extreme futility. It is costly in both time and money. However, so much pressure was put on OSHA that the agency has recently recognized the senselessness of its meat-ax approach. It has eliminated over 1,100 former unreasonable regulations and has prom-ised a more sensible approach in the future. Some of the regulations that have been revoked or modified are stan-dards that apply to U-shaped toilet seats, the type of wood used for portable ladders, and the height where fire extin-guishers are to be mounted.

Regulating the trucking industry has resulted in con-sumer price increases estimated at 20% of the cost.* Further-more, it effectively enforces by law a method of artificial pricing that should be governed by the American system of free enterprise based on competition.

In many cases productivity is being sabotaged for dubi-ous ecological values. Can we blame the man in the street for raising an eyebrow when he reads in the morning paper that work has halted on the Tellico Dam across the Little Tennes-see River to save 10,000 snail darters that have no economic value? By simple arithmetic this action could cost the tax-payers $11,600 for each snail darter.

*A.N. Wecksler, "The High Cost of Government Regulation." *Appliance Manufacturer*, February 1979.

Who's to Blame?

The obvious abuses by a government that has been elected for the purpose of ensuring our national welfare prompt the question: "Why, in a democratic form of government, do we permit these things to continue?" And if we look at this question objectively we are forced to admit that all of us, to a degree, are motivated by a spirit of self-interest. We have become mesmerized by the dubious benefits that have been permitted to trickle back in our direction. We are all for reductions in government spending as long as these reductions do not affect our private playground.

Few groups are more vocal about excess government spending than the American farmers. Yet they continue to accept government parities, artificial controls, and government funds for keeping productive acreage idle.

Industry, in general, claims to deplore government paternalism, but it often cries for government intervention when its stockholders begin hammering their fists on the desk of the Chairman of the Board.

A perfect example of this phenomenon is the American auto industry. On the one hand, its members complain about too much government intervention in matters like emission controls, safety equipment, and artificially created financing rates. Yet on the other hand they are pleading with the government for embargoes and tariffs to keep foreign competition off their collective backs. In the words of syndicated columnist Andy Rooney, "Is Chrysler for or against big government? If it's against it, I'd like to keep my billion dollars, thank you."

And how about the average American—the typical shoe salesman from Dubuque? If asked, he will claim to oppose government paternalism. Yet, if forced into a financial corner, he will probably readily accept amenities like unemployment insurance, food stamps, welfare benefits, and artificial pricing of commodities as long as they work in his favor. We all pay for this paternalistic welfarism. Idaho's congressman Steven S. Symms reported in a newsletter that in 1948, 24.2% of every dollar earned went for taxes. In 1957, 35.5%

went for taxes. By 1968, 39.2% went for taxes, and in 1979 a whopping 42% of every hard-earned dollar went for taxes.

Despite inability to attain national office, in the past 50 years the Socialist Party has been the most influential factor in our national economy. If you're inclined to challenge this statement, a check of the 1932 Socialist party platform will reveal that almost every item in that platform has by now been enacted into law.

Now let's take a look at the second leg of the three-legged stool mentioned earlier in this chapter.

Organized Labor

Few would deny that some of the occupational abuses conducted by management earlier in our history required and perhaps demanded some reforms. However, during the past several decades, organized labor has acquired gains out of all proportion to the additional productivity it has contributed.

Labor bought its ticket from our nation's politicians and it still hasn't cashed in on the final installment. Because of counterabuses following World War II, labor must share the responsibility for our current productivity lag.

The philosophy of many labor unions can best be summed up by some dialogue that took place on a "Meet the Press" TV interview almost 20 years ago. The program guest was the late John L. Lewis, who had just called a strike of United States coal miners during a period when fuel was in precariously short supply. A Maine newspaper columnist by the name of Mae Craig asked the labor leader how he could justify denying the nation the energy it so badly needed simply to acquire more money for his membership. The labor leader's reply was brief and to the point. "I'm elected to my office," he said, "to get the members of my organization as much money for as little work as possible. Now, if you want to talk about morality I'd suggest you get Billy Graham on your program."

The Teamsters' Union has opposed every step taken by the ICC for freer competition in the trucking industry. For obvious reasons, the union prefers the status quo to competition with independent haulers. More than a third of a century elapsed between the introduction of the diesel engine, and the time that the Brotherhood of Locomotive Firemen and Engineers finally agreed to eliminate the job of fireman. Then, of course, it was only on the basis of attrition.

Virtually every segment of industry is replete with the practice of featherbedding and work slowdowns. Horror stories of these practices are many and varied. They include carpenters who will not install prehung doors or sashes; painters who limit the size of paintbrushes and rollers; electricians who require a skilled craftsman to install a new light bulb; rigid insistence on recognition of seniority alone regardless of skill level; restricting duties; prohibition of labor-saving machines; excessive nonproductive downtime; and other occupational scams too numerous to mention.

The biggest portion of our national income is devoted to employee compensation. Despite this fact, labor has consistently pressed ahead for higher and higher wages with little or no concern for productivity. Twenty-five years ago, 64% of our national income consisted of employee compensation. The figure now stands at 75%. Because of this imbalance, labor productivity is now approaching zero growth. Yet the goose that lays the golden eggs continues to get squeezed.

Even the union workers who enjoy these unprecedented benefits are becoming aware that this condition cannot go on indefinitely. A recent survey by Opinion Research Corporation found that 61% of the union workers who were polled agreed with the statement: "Wages paid in this country make it difficult for the United States to compete in world markets."

Labor *must* come to grips with the unpleasant fact that wage increases can be justified only by increases in productivity. There is no other way.

Where Do We Go from Here?

From the standpoint of industry, the most frustrating thing about these problems is that many of them seem to defy any practical solution. Too many of our tax legislators simply don't understand business and what it takes to remain competitive. Some of our nation's most powerful congressmen have virtually no business experience. Some of them, in fact, don't even seem to understand how the free enterprise system works. In addition to congressional hostility, the business community is seemingly overwhelmed by the elements in our society who would have us tax business further on the grounds that it has an endless supply of money.

Actions to curb the demands of organized labor have been similarly unsuccessful. Labor isn't about to give up the gains it has acquired in the past half century. Why should it? Its formula has been enormously successful; so successful that its present attitude toward labor-management negotiations usually centers on a policy of "What's mine is mine and what's yours is negotiable."

Where then do we look to alleviate the crisis that threatens the very lifeblood of our economy?

Fortunately there is one segment where huge potential for improvement exists and where dramatic corrective action can be taken. This area is management—the third leg of the three-legged stool—where huge deficiencies also occur.

two

Management's Problem Areas

According to an epigram known as Jones's Law, "The man who can smile when everything is going wrong has already found someone to blame it on." Perhaps this may explain why a sizable portion of the business community still can manage an occasional smile in spite of staggering government regulations and seemingly unconscionable demands by organized labor. Certainly there's adequate blame to be distributed between both of these entities.

Yet a closer look at the situation demands that we pose the question: "Is it fair, or even accurate, for management (the third leg of the three-legged stool) to sit back on its diminishing assets and piously heap all of its accusations and criticisms against every segment of the industrial structure except itself?"

Can management hold itself blameless when it allegedly deplores government intervention yet becomes a warm and cozy partner to big government to suit its own purpose? Can it sincerely complain so bitterly against union encroachment of its prerogatives when it does little to provide workers with the same benefits produced by organized labor until union organizers begin camping on its doorstep?

The difficulties faced by management are numerous

and varied. But on the basis of a lifetime of observation into the inner workings of numerous industries, I feel compelled to state that the reason for most of management's problems can be readily identified by a long, hard look into a full-length mirror.

I make this statement with the full realization that this book will be read primarily by management people, and human nature being what it is, personal criticism is seldom received with anything approaching wild enthusiasm. All I ask is that you keep an open mind about the management shortcomings discussed in this chapter and the methods by which these failings can be alleviated, which will be presented later in the book. If I can convince you that you can manage your company without outside assistance and then get you sufficiently upset that you'll go back to your plant or office and do something about it, this book will have served its ultimate purpose.

Let's look first at a few personal management characteristics that have weakened management's image as a symbol of leadership and ultimately resulted in decreased productivity.

Accentuating the Negative

Many of today's younger businessmen probably never heard the popular song of a previous era that advises us to accentuate the positive. Furthermore, a sizable number of their counterparts from an earlier generation seem to have forgotten the words of wisdom that were so popular on the Lucky Strike Hit Parade.

One of the most prevalent forms of negative thinking among members of today's business community is *procrastination.* Management all too often fails to face up to unpleasant facts that, if confronted squarely, could actually turn disadvantages into advantages. Evading a fact doesn't change it!

There are few things in this life that are as constant as change and the need to adapt to it. Yet American industry has shown a marked reluctance to adopt new methods, modify obsolete procedures, and take advantage of modern technology.

In a large manufacturing firm, recommendations were made to modify the assembly line. It was estimated that under the proposed procedure production could be increased by 16% with the same number of employees currently in the workforce.

The suggested change had the blessing of the workers, the union, and, indeed, management itself. However, the chief executive resisted immediate implementation on the grounds that it was during the summer vacation period and training employees for the revised operation could be better accomplished when the full workforce was on deck.

Later in the year the proposal was presented again. This time it was vetoed because the assembly line was operating at full capacity and it was felt that the 16 hours downtime required to make the changes would impede current production.

The following spring, due largely to delays in carrying out the original plan, the union had some second thoughts and began making noises about the project constituting a work speedup for its membership. The chief executive initially capitulated to union objections, but a year later was able to convince the union leaders that the modification would be beneficial to all concerned.

The story has a happy ending, or unhappy—depending on how you look at it. Implementation was finally accomplished almost *two years* after the proposal was first introduced, and the company was later able to document savings of $216,000 a year under the new procedure. Or, put another way, because of the initial procrastination, the company lost $432,000!

One of the primary requisites for managerial effectiveness, in my opinion, is the ability to distinguish between the important and the unimportant. Often, as in the case above, huge company profits can be literally sabotaged by a reluctance to recognize true priorities. Another failing on the part of many managements today is a marked propensity—probably generated by increased worker's rights and union strength—to substitute appeasement for true leadership when making tough decisions.

It is not necessary for anyone to revert back to the role of the dominant executive that was prevalent during the 1930s. Competent help today will not work for an executive who sets himself up as a one-man band.

On the other hand, it's absolutely essential for management to assume the role of leadership when it comes to making controversial decisions. This credo, which is sadly lacking in many organizations today, must be instilled and practiced by all members of management.

We Know You're There—Your Name Is on the Time Card

It used to be standard procedure for the chief executive to make a daily visit through the plant. In the course of this inspection he got to know many of the employees by name, and it was not uncommon for him to solicit and receive valuable input concerning shop conditions and problems.

Due in part to the complexity of modern industry, coupled with the proliferation of various support functions, this practice has become as extinct as the nickel candy bar.

The calculated isolation of top management from the people who perform the work can best be illustrated by the incredible fact that at a large manufacturing plant, it was necessary for the chief executive to call the plant superintendent on the telephone for an appointment to tour his own plant.

Top managers are very shortsighted not to recognize that their most valuable company asset is the people who make their product or perform their services. To make matters even worse, this industrial isolationism is not confined solely to the relationship between staff management and production workers. It extends to first-line supervisors, foremen, support specialists, and even members of middle management. It's as if an invisible line were drawn at some point in the table of organization that makes it slightly unethical for top management to fraternize with the rabble who occupy a lower rung on the administrative ladder.

Numerous surveys have been conducted among shop personnel on the subject of communications. And invariably the same complaint is heard: "Sure, those people upstairs tell us everything they want us to know. *But they never listen to our problems!*" It's almost as if top management were saying: "Don't bother us with your petty problems. We've got *important* things to worry about."

Realistically, however, few managers would deny that one of their most important problems is to establish and maintain good communications with the people who produce the company's goods and services. This includes dialogue both up and down.

Disorganized Organization

The wrongheaded superspecialization that can result from excessive preoccupation with organization charts and printed job descriptions is strangling American industry and costing the business community billions of dollars each year.

I'm not denying the necessity for organization charts and printed job descriptions as general guidelines for organizational relationships and employee responsibilities. But when the people involved begin regarding these items as something akin to the Sermon on the Mount, the organization can be in for big trouble.

I don't think the organization chart was ever devised that presented an accurate picture of the organizational relationships of each and every employee. And this goes double when it comes to printed job descriptions geared to a position rather than to the individual who performs the work. Let's face it, any employees worth the ink it takes to sign their paychecks are more than a totality of facts and figures designed for the purpose of fitting people into convenient job slots. They are individuals. And as individuals they possess traits that in all probability make them effective in several different job categories. To maneuver them into stereotyped roles simply to satisfy the bloodless requirements of an organization chart is not only bad business but an insult to the intelligence, initiative, and morale of fellow human beings who might, with a little help, develop into key members of the organization.

The problems caused by preoccupation with organization charts have been further compounded in recent years by the addition of various support units like safety, industrial engineering, and training, which have been neatly sandwiched into the organizational structure.

In view of the complex nature of modern industry these support functions are, admittedly, necessary. However, in many instances their effectiveness is complicated by vague organizational relationships and dubious areas of authority. Often these areas of authority, either by accident or design, tend to intrude excessively into production activities and create problems that would not have existed had the lines of authority been more sensibly delineated.

Full Pay for Part-Time Work

Low productivity in industry is a condition that comes about by failure to apply manpower, money, and machines in the most effective manner possible with the resources and expertise that are currently available.

If we accept this statement as true, a company could expect to attain 100% productivity with all of these factors working at top performance. (Actually, this statement could be an oversimplification, since improvements in methods, processing, or techniques could increase production to a point where a figure in excess of 100% productivity was possible. In this case top performers under the modified procedure would represent the 100% figure.)

Unfortunately, since business and industry are fraught with unforeseen problems and uncertainties, it is usually unrealistic to expect attainment of 100% productivity. Accordingly, business must then decide what lesser percentage figure represents an acceptable level, and at which point the people charged with production activities might be well advised to either develop some improvement or start circulating their résumés.

Productivity expectation varies by industry, but some basic guidelines put an acceptable productivity level at 80%, with 50% falling into the area of unsatisfactory.

The reasons for unsatisfactory productivity at the manufacturing level are many and varied. They consist primarily of a simple failure to obtain a full day's work for a full day's pay. They include unscheduled and prolonged work breaks, lack of shop discipline, sporadic machine loading, poor scheduling, and inadequate processing.

In other cases, and these occur with alarming frequency, production is impaired by factors that are, or should be, the responsibility of management. These include things like poorly maintained incentive systems, inadequate base pay rates, poor methods, lack of equipment utilization, inadequate maintenance, poor setup, and improper tooling.

Lack of shop control, generated by inadequate systems or excessive paperwork, also has an adverse effect on production. Poor inventory controls take an additional bite out of the productivity pie.

All these problem areas have two things in common. They create difficulties at the operations level and impair productivity. The difference between companies that consistently show a high rate of earnings and those that operate in red ink frequently depends on how conscientiously these conditions can be monitored and remedied.

There They Go. I Must Hasten after Them, for I Am Their Leader!

During the past several decades the working conditions of virtually every job category in America have improved. The one exception to this is *first-line supervisors*. They and they alone have lost most of their former authority and prestige and have simultaneously been saddled with additional work and responsibility. In return they have watched the pay spread between themselves and their subordinates dwindle away and finally, in some cases, disappear altogether.

This drastic change has been caused by a number of factors, not the least of which has been the growth in workers' rights and the creation of various support factors like safety, training, and industrial engineering, which often tend to intrude into the foreman's former prerogatives to a prohibitive degree.

Yet despite these altogether logical causes, the foreman is still the *only* member of management who has direct contact with the workers on a day-to-day basis. Foremen are still charged with being the chief motivating force in attaining acceptable production. They are the buffer zone in a three-sided tug-of-war between labor, management, and the union. In addition to this the foreman is expected to be a record keeper, mother or father image, administrator of discipline, amateur psychologist, labor management expert, work coordinator, and training specialist.

In return for these services many industrial leaders keep foremen in the dark about changes in company policy, fail to invite them to staff meetings, summarily countermand their decisions, rarely consider them for promotion to middle management, and hold them responsible for standards they've had no control over developing. Is it any wonder that, confronted with a no-win situation of this type, many foremen throw up their hands in disgust?

The marked deterioration of the foreman as a symbol of leadership can be illustrated by an incident that occurred at a midwestern auto assembly plant. A foreman at this plant, whom I'll refer to as Bill Young, was trained like many of his contemporaries on the premise that a basic criterion for a good manager is the ability to obtain production from employees under his jurisdiction.

In his zeal to keep his unit operating with an acceptable degree of efficiency, Young on three separate occasions was involved in altercations with the United Auto Workers union. In one of these instances, a charge of harassing an employee was the subject of a formal grievance. The charge was subsequently dropped by the hearing officer and Young's superiors. Nevertheless, he was required to submit to embarrassing questioning about his motives and general attitudes toward subordinates.

Because of the problems he had encountered in trying to enforce discipline in his unit, Young now readily admits he has recently found it easier to overlook some irregularities than to plunge headlong into another confrontation with the union and top management. Sad to state, Young's story is not an isolated case. It is occurring daily in all segments of American industry.

This major problem will be discussed in more detail in Chapter 5.

The Fast-Fading Fashion of Industrial Accountability

There's an old administrative axiom that states: "No problem is unsolvable if it can be pushed over on the other fellow's desk." This policy, which has long been the credo of government and politics, has unfortunately become more and more prevalent in the business community. Pledges and promises to perform a service, deliver an order, keep an appointment, maintain a deadline, or operate within a budget all too often seem to be meaningless commitments that freely translated mean: "I might do this, providing it's convenient, everything works out just right, and nothing more important develops."

The end result for those naive enough to gear their own activities to the other person's promises is irritability, wasted man-hours, financial distress, and often a monumental loss in customer goodwill, generated by a chain reaction of reduced productivity and broken promises that extends through the entire manufacturing process.

Lack of accountability, unfortunately, is not confined to the auto mechanic who promises delivery of a car by a deadline he has no intention of honoring. It exists throughout the entire business chain of command. Some of the most chronic abusers, in fact, are executives high in the administrative echelon who, because of their rank, feel they are immune to the accountability standards they request from subordinates.

An intense need exists for some solid guidelines to insure accountability standards for every member of the organization. This is not an impossible feat. A proven method to develop and insure accountability will be presented later in this book.

W. F. Rockwell, Jr., former chairman of the board at Rockwell International, appraises accountability as follows: "Good men not only want their contributions measured, they insist on it . . . mediocre men *must* be held accountable; good men *want* to be held accountable."

Who Sells Productivity to the Sales Division?

Most companies have, at one time or another, initiated various types of performance improvement programs or cost-cutting measures. Unfortunately, many of these have been of the meat-ax variety and consist, in effect, of a flat order to cut expenses across the board by a fixed percentage. This strategy effectively permits areas of marked inefficiency to whittle off the required volume of fat with practically no ill effects, while generating a sizable flow of blood from departments that have attempted to operate over the years with a minimum degree of waste. Other programs, of a more selective nature, have managed to remove enough lard from the operation to make the depressing statistics a bit more palatable.

Nearly all these plans have one thing in common. They are directed, oddly enough, primarily against operations—an area that even in normal times is, or should be, watched carefully by all levels of supervision.

To a lesser degree, typically when nonproduction workers begin stumbling over their checkerboards, some type of program may also be devised to upgrade efficiency among maintenance workers and office personnel. However, there is one entity in the industrial structure that consistently receives little or no attention by top management in the matter of developing improved operational procedures. This is the sales division, which is frequently permitted to operate with few restraints and fewer basic guidelines.

The potential for improvement in the sales division by application of modern management methods is tremendous, providing the department can be coordinated with the manufacturing process instead of functioning as an isolated unit that is permitted to make its own rules and march to the beat of its own drummer. This will be discussed further in Chapter 10.

The Board of Directors—What Does It Direct?

Ask the average man in the street to describe a typical member of the board of directors, and chances are he'll portray a pompous, middle-aged, slightly overweight individual who has little knowledge of the actual workings of the company and has been appointed to his position for the basic purpose of rubber-stamping such policies as might be set forth by top management. And, unfortunately for today's industry, this stereotyped image is frequently as accurate as any definition that has yet been developed.

Lesser management positions like those in industrial relations, personnel management, or systems and procedures analysis have developed over a period of years into virtual professions. Not so with the board of directors. If anything, its function has atrophied over the years.

In an era that has been marked by computer technology and streamlined management methods, it is something of a paradox that the people who are directly responsible for keeping America's corporate wheels in motion have been permitted to pursue a course so completely resistant to change. Yet, with some notable exceptions, today's so-called space-age director is little changed from his counterpart in the Victorian era.

If the above analysis seems harsh, consider that one of the Penn Central's former directors explained his company's fiasco by stating in a rare moment of candor: "I don't think anyone was aware it was that close to collapse."

There's got to be a better way to operate, and fortunately there is! A proven method of making the board of directors a viable asset to management, rather than a group of prestigious figureheads who meet once a month for the purpose of nodding with executive palsy on an appropriate cue, will be presented in Chapter 7.

Low Wages Do Not Mean Low Costs

Today's bankruptcy courts are literally crammed with firms that have doggedly adhered to the erroneous principle of cheap labor. This is not to imply that the woes of the American businessman can automatically be eliminated by the simple expedient of giving all employees a 20% raise. The secret lies in the not-too-unreasonable premise that management has a right to expect a fair day's work for a fair day's pay.

Indisputable surveys have consistently indicated that strict adherence to minimum wage scales invariably results in less than minimum performance. Conversely, employees who are carefully selected and given work conditions that are conducive to pride of accomplishment in their work will, on a dollar-for-unit basis, improve their productivity far in excess of the additional wages expended.

Put another way: For average wages you get average productivity. For high wages one would think that you'd get high productivity. But you don't. You get *unusually* high productivity.

I can personally cite hundreds of cases where profits for the firm and wages for its workers were both increased *providing* the wage increases were geared to better production based on meaningful incentives and realistic work measurement.

Long-Range Planning, Short-Range Results

A fashionable phrase in today's management lexicon is "long-range planning." Properly designed and executed, long-range planning is a valuable tool to business and industry. Too often, however, these programs are poorly conceived, badly developed, and improperly carried out. The low rate of success stems from three basic factors: lack of involvement, lack of communication, and lack of commitment.

More often than not, the initial enthusiasm with which a program is developed appears to level off after a while. Then, sustained by little more than an intense spirit of apathy, the program withers on the vine and finally dies from lack of attention.

Long-range planning without vigorous follow-through is an exercise in futility. It must be nurtured and cared for by the people who designed it. There is no other way.

What Can We Do about It?

I'm acutely aware of the fact that up to this point my observations concerning the shortcomings of management have been extremely harsh. Perhaps this might be a good place to interject that the problems outlined in this chapter do not apply to every organization. I'll go a step further and state that if *all* the abuses cited here applied to any single organization, that firm would have long since been dissolved by the tender mercies of our nation's bankruptcy courts.

Nevertheless, as I have observed in an untold number of companies over the years, it's a good bet that some, or perhaps even *many,* of the counterproductive practices cited in this chapter exist in the work world of the vast majority of the people who read this book.

I base this judgment on the fact that the thoughts expressed in the preceding pages not only consist of my own observations, but also represent the input contributed by a sizable group of top management executives who were surveyed on this subject.

Admittedly, not all of the problems of management could be covered in a single book. Sometimes I think a full compilation of management's difficulties and problems might fill a sizable portion of the Library of Congress. However, some of the most outstanding management problems have now been cited. The balance of this volume will consist of ways in which these and other industrial shortcomings can be alleviated.

three

Increasing Production Through Work Measurement

The only safeguard of order and discipline in the modern world is a standardized worker with interchangeable parts. That would solve the entire problem of management.

Jean Giraudoux, The Madwoman of Chaillot

The acid test of the next decade that will separate the major leaguer from the sandlot player is productivity management. Far too often the American manager thinks that to increase productivity significantly, much capital spending or many changes in technology are required. This myth must be dispelled. There are just too many productivity improvement programs available today that enable management to reduce costs in the nation's factories and offices without resorting to large capital appropriations for investing in new machinery and equipment, or implementing comprehensive research and development programs.

Productivity improvements must begin by getting back to the basics. And one way to start is by utilizing the various

means at our disposal to improve the productivity of labor—
our nation's greatest resource.

Why Is Work Measurement Important?

Work measurement programs and wage incentives are two
of the basic management tools used to improve labor productivity. The elements of any successful labor control program incorporate standards of performance benchmarks.
An industrial fact of life is that over 60% of the manufacturing companies in this country do not have any formalized
standards of accountability for employees. They operate simply on a day-work basis with little or no record of what their
employees should produce and consequently have no yardsticks for their supervision.

Too often, management does not recognize and appreciate the fact that without formalized yardsticks for first-
line supervisors, it has no means of measuring supervisory
performance. Simple, formalized yardsticks of work measurement and accountability can practically guarantee any
company a 15% minimum direct labor cost reduction. If
those companies want to go a step further and utilize the
wage incentive principle, they can increase production a
minimum of 40%.

These are not wild figures that have been plucked out of
the air. They can be indisputably documented by studies
made over the years. If anything, they may tend to somewhat
understate the benefits of this important management tool.

Wage Incentives: Do They Really Work?

An *Industrial Engineering* magazine article entitled "Work
Measurement and Wage Incentives" by Mitchell Fein is even
more optimistic regarding productivity improvements. In
the article, Mr. Fein tells of a survey to show the relationship
of incentives to productivity, and it indicated that changing
from no measurement to incentives increased productivity
an average of 51.5%. My own experience bears this out.

Figured by anybody's yardstick, this is one whale of an improvement! In fact, with figures like this going for them, one cannot help but ponder the question: "If wage incentives are all this good, why isn't everyone using them?"

The lack of enthusiasm, unfortunately, is often based on reports from other companies where the incentive concept has been tried and has failed. However, in most cases pessimistic managers totally ignore the undeniable fact that most unsuccessful incentive plans fail for a variety of reasons, any of which could be overcome by the application of meaningful controls and sound management principles.

Work standards, like the incentive plans that often accompany this management device, seldom die of natural causes, but rather from neglect, malnutrition, and fatal abuse. They must be constantly monitored or the results can be disastrous.

Make no mistake! Realistic work measurement and incentive principles can be developed and effectively applied for any operation in any company. These include materials handling, maintenance, warehouse operation, office and clerical work, drafting, engineering, and administrative management.

In an era of fierce competition the failure of any company to exercise the principles of work measurement is like embarking on a trip around the world without a compass or road map. And this goes double for incentives.

A Tool to Build Profitability

Of the many tasks performed by the industrial engineering department, none is more sensitive to labor relations—and few are more significant to profits—than the development and implementation of wage incentive plans. The reason this task is so sensitive to labor relations is that it deals directly with the worker's take-home pay, and it is significant to bottom-line results because of the profit impact wage incentives can have on reducing labor costs.

For these basic reasons, the tasks of developing, installing, and maintaining a wage incentive plan must be approached on a sound and consistent basis. Equal importance should be given to all elements of wage incentive development and plant maintenance.

The use of sound basic methods, appropriate, well-engineered measurement data, tight administrative control procedures, and clearly defined operational guidelines must be carefully weighed to implement the plan properly. A neglect of just one of the parts will cause the deterioration of the wage incentive plan.

In designing base rates and work standards, a high degree of cooperation and understanding is necessary by both labor and management. Active participation by both parties in drawing up the wage incentive plan is essential. Problems often develop from subtle changes in procedures or performance that, if undetected or ignored, tend to distort standards that were originally designed in good faith. This loosening of standards on some jobs and tightening on others creates a situation where employees can work hard on jobs where it is easy to acquire extra earnings and loaf on jobs where these earnings cannot easily be achieved.

The development of the wage incentive plan must be kept simple and straightforward so that everyone can understand its principles and application. This applies especially to indoctrinating the worker on the shop floor. Far too often management feels that the plan, in order to be effective, must be complex, with variable formulas and productivity factors to cover all the conditions.

Companies also make the fatal mistake of circumventing the plan's design by substituting economic rhetoric in the belief that it will induce the employee to become more productive. However, all the stereotyped pep talks and management platitudes that ever came out of an industrial relations textbook are not going to stimulate much adrenaline in the veins of a factory worker who's worried about where next month's car payment is coming from. Yet show him in simple terms how he can earn the needed money in the same number of hours that he's presently working and you're getting into a principle of economics with which he can empathize.

Regaining Control: The Lost Art of Management

Without some form of work measurement, be it wage incentives or measured day work, management never really grasps control of the corporate steering wheel. The ship is sailing, but the course is often charted by employees and shop stewards. Work measurement properly applied puts the control back in the hands of management, where it belongs. It forces management either to take charge or in essence to hand over the keys to the front door, because in all likelihood the workers or the union have been running the place anyway.

From an employee relations position, the average worker would much rather be associated with a company that knows which direction it is going and has "hands on" control over costs to meet competition than with a firm that constantly has to test the water before jumping in with both feet. Cost reduction through work measurement and operational improvement flows directly to the bottom line and can have an immeasurable effect on profitability—especially for the firm that has not yet adopted this profit control tool.

Why Incentive Plans Fail

There are many reasons why even the best-made incentive plans fail. Any wage incentive system can go awry, and targets can be missed when the plan is poorly conceived. To accomplish specific results when developing a wage incentive plan, management must avoid these classic pitfalls.

1. *Misunderstanding the output-earnings relationship.* The employee as well as his or her supervisor must understand how much output is required to earn incentive pay. A vague understanding of a work standard is one of the principal hazards that cause an incentive plan to fail.

2. *Placing a ceiling on earnings.* There should be no ceilings on earnings. When this occurs, production is often pegged, and industrial engineers have a tendency to set loose rates. Checks and balances can be incorporated into a proper wage incentive plan to control creeping changes.

3. *Employing haphazard work measurement.* Work measurement should be appropriately developed for the operation and is the cornerstone for any wage incentive plan. Without proper work measurement, the credibility of the plan is questioned, and both labor and management will become disenchanted. You can't perform a major operation with Band-aids.

4. *Deploying complicated earnings calculations.* The calculation of incentive earnings must be kept simple if the worker is to know the relationship of effort applied to the realization of extra pay. Intricate formulas and earnings calculations will discourage a worker from producing more output in order to earn more pay.

5. *Using incentives as a panacea.* Management must take an active role at the outset in making the plan work. Too often managers feel that the wage incentive plan is a panacea and substitute for their involvement. This is perhaps the greatest pitfall that causes the demise of most wage incentive plans.

6. *Not having the house in order.* Work flows must be balanced, and the house must be in order. The disorderly house in this context is poor equipment, shortages of materials, and other factors that cause incentive workers to lose their extra pay. Production also declines when these problems are not corrected, and this is the first step toward guaranteed wages—more aptly called "pay average."

7. *Inconsistent work standards.* Work standards must be consistent, and the roller-coaster effect minimized. If standards are loose, extra worker efforts will be applied to generate more earnings. If they are tight, employees will drag their work out, and production will be minimized. Tight standards evoke a clamoring workforce. And this is a critical issue that causes labor problems. Both of these conditions must be corrected immediately.

8. *Using amateurs as incentive plan architects.* The wage incentive plan should not be developed by amateurs. Using inexperienced personnel with a limited background as architects to design the plan is like putting a seaman apprentice

in control of the flagship. This will only lead to problems of immense proportions.

9. *Applying low base rates.* Don't develop a plan around a poor base rate structure. Constructing a plan around low base rates in hopes that a high earnings incentive opportunity will correct the situation is only postponing the inevitable. Sooner or later there is a day of reckoning. Base rates must be equitable. An incentive plan should not be used as a substitute for fair base rates.

10. *Not letting labor participate.* The input of both parties should be considered in the plan's design. Active participation of both labor and management is essential in developing checks and balances to make the plan successful. Appropriate language must be incorporated to protect both parties.

11. *Indiscriminate rate cutting.* The plan must incorporate language that states there will be no indiscriminate rate cutting. However, the wage incentive plan must spell out situations where standards will be adjusted to conform with changes in methods. Procedures should also be developed to handle rate disputes.

12. *Overlooking the management audit.* Work standards should be audited periodically by the industrial engineering department. No plan should be implemented without provisions for auditing production standards. This is management's assurance that creeping changes can be controlled.

13. *Poorly trained supervisors.* Supervisors must be properly trained in the fundamentals of wage incentives if the plan is to be successful. As management's front-line representatives they must know how the standards are established, be thoroughly familiar with the language and contractual provisions, and must establish a close liaison with the industrial engineering department. It is this level of management that determines how successful wage incentives will be.

14. *Negotiating work standards.* Work standards should not be negotiated to quell worker discontent or put out fires. To do so is the same as negotiating away productivity. If standards are not representative of the operation being performed, they should be investigated and adjusted on an en-

gineered basis, not at the third step of the grievance proce-dure by those who can't take the heat of the kitchen.

15. *Using incentives as a substitute.* Once the incentive plan is installed, management worries are not over, contrary to popular belief. Incentives must be properly maintained or problems will surely develop and deteriorate the wage incentive plan. Appropriate methods, well-developed work standards, proper documentation, and tight administrative control procedures are essential to implement the plan properly.

Components of a Successful Wage Incentive Plan

The six basic ingredients required for developing a successful incentive plan must include guidelines for implementing methods improvements, establishing base rates, developing work standards, calculating earnings, providing an incentive opportunity, and creating a harmonious relationship between labor and management. The six components are as follows:

1. *Methods and operational improvements.* A comprehensive methods analysis should be made of each operation before developing work standards. The methods analysis phase of the wage incentive plan should not be limited to just the direct labor areas where incentive standards are to be installed, but should include nonincentive operations as well.

A full-scope investigation of each direct labor operation should cover its relationship to other activities within and outside the department where standards will be installed. This would include production planning, scheduling, and materials control functions. The indirect support areas such as maintenance and materials handling should also be reviewed for their service effectiveness and their impact on direct labor operations.

Too often management, in its eagerness to realize immediate productivity improvements, will only touch the surface when improving methods. Managers should recognize that when operations have gone basically untouched for a period of time, they offer tremendous potential for cost savings. The key areas of investigation in a methods analysis should be work flow improvements, work station redesign, and production reporting techniques.

2. *Appropriate base rates.* Base rates must be equitably structured by job evaluation or other acceptable means. An incentive plan with a high earnings multiplier should not be used as a substitute for paying a fair hourly base rate. Hourly earnings must be in relationship to both effort and productive output; the concept of a fair day's pay for a fair day's work must prevail.

3. *Engineered work standards.* Work standards must be realistic and attainable, and they should be expressed in terms the worker can understand. Appropriate documentation must be established so that methods are clearly spelled out. This is especially important for conducting an operations audit or investigating a rate challenge.

4. *Methods of calculating earnings.* To fully benefit from a wage incentive plan, both the worker and management must understand how incentive earnings are calculated. Provisions for nonstandard or unusual job conditions must be drafted concerning materials, equipment, employee training, and job transfers. The method by which incentive earnings are paid must be fully defined. There is nothing more demoralizing to a worker than misunderstanding the program and getting substantially less take-home pay than anticipated.

5. *Sufficient earnings opportunity.* Management must assure labor that it will provide an incentive opportunity by keeping the equipment running, having materials available, and having jobs set up ready to operate. Work flows must be balanced, and any delays beyond the worker's control must be minimized. Also, the earnings opportunity must not be capped with an upper limit. A half-hearted attempt by management to provide an incentive opportunity will only disillusion workers. The coverage factor must also be adequate if management or labor is to realize any appreciable benefit from embarking on a wage incentive plan.

6. *Harmonious labor-management relations.* Good labor re-

lations are the nucleus of a successful wage incentive plan. When each party acts in good faith and is cognizant of the other's concern, the plan should take off. Most incentive problems are people-related and do not result from technical shortcomings.

Establishing Control with Measured Day Work

Measured day work is a form of management control. It is used as a labor control system by companies to measure individual worker output and the total performance of an area. Measured day work differs from a wage incentive system in the areas of take-home earnings and management control. Unlike under an incentive system, the workers' income is not dependent on output.

Measured day-work standards are generally used in areas where no measurement exists or the operation is highly automated. The selection of measured day work over wage incentives usually occurs when an operation is new and less standardized, or management becomes disenchanted with wage incentives.

The output from machine- or process-controlled operations is dependent not on worker effort but on the equipment itself. Employee attention time, however, is very important to the equipment's operation. The opportunity for increasing productivity with measured day-work aids is enhanced by worker effort or new methods and equipment.

Principles of Work Measurement

For the full advantages of a work measurement plan to be realized, its development and installation must be based on sound principles. The ten basic principles for getting the most productivity from a measured day-work plan are as follows:

1. The front-line supervisor must be capable of super-

vising people through human relations skills and good management techniques.

2. The supervisor must be a take-charge person and directly supervise people in his or her area of responsibility. Group leaders or assistants should not have direct authority for the department and must not separate the supervisor from the workers.

3. The span of control must be reasonable and the number of employees supervised limited. The complexity of the operation, the type of work performed, and the geographic area in which the employees work must be considered in determining the number of workers to be supervised. The span can vary from 15 to 40 employees.

4. The supervisor must be held accountable for his or her people and assigned area of responsibility. The supervisor's primary responsibility is to be in the area and assure that employees work productively, using prescribed methods and meeting quality requirements.

5. Work standards should be established so that worker performance can be evaluated. The supervisor should give corrective assistance and counseling to the worker not meeting these standards. The department's cost effectiveness is a direct result of the actual output of the people. This performance reflects the capability of the supervisor in meeting goals and schedules developed from the measurement data applied in the area.

6. Work standards must be accurate and kept up to date in the departments being measured. They should be established by recognized industrial engineering techniques and include documentation, and they must be periodically audited to conform to any changes.

7. The supervisor must review and approve all work standards to be used in his or her area of responsibility. The supervisor must be convinced of the fairness and accuracy of the measurement data applied. Any disagreements between the supervisor and the industrial engineer should be resolved by higher management.

8. The workers should know the work standards in each

section under measurement. The standards may be published on an activity record prepared daily by the employee or posted to a routing sheet, depending on the type of operation controlled. The employees in the department should know what is expected of them if labor performance is to be significantly improved.

9. Nonstandard conditions are the responsibility of the supervisor, and unless these conditions are corrected, they detract from labor performance. The supervisor must correct conditions such as machines not in repair, materials or tools not available, or extra operations required.

10. Labor performance reports should be provided to the supervisor on a timely basis to establish management control. Reports should be available to the supervisor as soon as practical upon the completion of the work period.

Benefits for Management and Labor

There are certain advantages to the implementation of a measured day-work system. From the employee's perspective, the work measurement plan provides job satisfaction, recognition, and security. Other advantages also surface. The principal benefits to the company are numerous and extend from a more cost-effective operation to better managerial control. Supervision also adopts a more identifiable leadership role, perhaps more by necessity than choice. A listing of the benefits achieved by measured day work follows.

For the Employee

- Job security is more evident through effective utilization of time and equipment. Downtime is generally reduced and delays are minimized.
- In many cases the employee's job is made easier, especially when new methods are introduced, equipment is improved, or hand tools are provided.

- Personal satisfaction is gained by a sense of accomplishment when recording and displaying good individual performance. The employee is aware that management is appraising his or her performance.
- The plan absolves the employee from any blame for conditions affecting productivity that are beyond personal control.
- It assures the employee that he or she is receiving fair and impartial treatment in relation to other employees.

For the Company

- Measured day work provides better control of the labor cost and creates an interest in productivity. It places appropriate emphasis on minimizing nonproductive delays, unplanned work, and other factors that lower productivity.
- It aids technological progress and stimulates effort toward more automation. After the measured day-work plan is installed, increased productivity in each succeeding year must come from improved equipment and methods, not from increased worker effort.
- It provides a sound basis for strengthening supervision because, unlike the wage incentive program, it requires the supervisor to provide the stimulus for generating good operating performance.
- It greatly improves labor relations. The employees are handled impartially and know what is expected of them. Employees requiring assistance can be counseled or retrained, and disciplinary action is minimal.
- It enables the company to accurately determine operational costs and setup charges that are vital for estimating, pricing, and establishing economical means of manufacturing.

- It provides a basis for improving production scheduling, streamlining customer service, and reducing manufacturing costs. The end result allows a company to improve sales capacity and enhance its profit structure.
- It increases operational flexibility and equipment utilization by providing a productivity climate for real change. Experienced operators can be assigned to key production equipment where needed, within job classifications or labor grades, without adjustments or changes to base rates or wage earnings.
- It simplifies paperwork and payroll accounting transactions because employees are paid a day rate.

In conclusion, the principal advantage of developing a work measurement plan for the nonincentive operation is putting control back in the hands of management where it belongs. Such a plan also enhances labor-management relations, strengthens the supervisor, and casts him or her as a front-line representative of management.

Work measurement provides the supervisor with a cost avoidance device and leadership tool. It brings this position to the forefront and solidifies the supervisor's role as a productivity manager. And the plan makes it possible to supervise from a position of strength—not weakness.

Industrial Engineering: Direct Link to Productivity

Industrial engineering represents different things to different companies and at various levels of the same company. Regardless of the meaning and variety of activity, however, industrial engineering strives for similar objectives, employing common methods and performing a like range of related activities.

Industrial engineering assumes a number of specialized roles within the organization. In labor performance control, it is engaged in work measurement, job evaluation, methods improvement, plant and work station layout, and wage incentives. In unit cost control, it includes equipment justification, machine operating efficiency, materials utilization, budgetary controls, and overhead expense. And in plant facilities engineering, industrial engineering involves plant maintenance, facilities planning, and plant capacity.

Management Expectations

It is important for management to understand that the budgetary cost of industrial engineering operations is not an expense, but is in reality an investment in economical production capable of high multiple return. From my experience, a good industrial engineering operation should offer a return of approximately five times the cost of the department during the first year, four times the cost during the second year, and not less than three times the cost each year thereafter. It is equally important to recognize that the industrial engineer is not an individual who arrives on the scene with ready-made solutions to all the company's productivity problems. Rather, these solutions must come as a result of investigation, examination, and careful analysis.

Mission and Structure

Generally speaking, the strength of industrial engineering should be at the plant or division level so as to provide the autonomy, responsibility, and accountability that are needed. The two basic objectives of industrial engineering in any company large or small are to design and establish efficient programs for controlling production costs, and to develop and implement sound programs for increased productivity, thereby reducing production costs.

The size and structure of the industrial engineering department in a given plant or division is dependent on the size of the direct labor force as well as on the complexity and number of operations involved. Obviously it is influenced strongly by company objectives such as a common practice of intentionally staffing so as to provide a training pool for developing first-line supervisors, or on the other hand, operating the industrial engineering functions at the bare minimum for maintenance of existing programs. Incidentally, the industrial engineering department is singularly well suited to serve the training and development function; however, cost reduction is its main business. I have seen in countless instances how the application of tested ideas for profit improvement can provide invaluable help to companies in meeting competition and increasing sales and profits, providing the engineering department operates with a degree of subtlety and restraint.

The role of the industrial engineering department is, at best, often somewhat adversary. All too often the presence of the industrial engineer is resented by supervisors. For industrial engineers to be effective, supervisors must be convinced that the engineers' sole purpose is to function as supervision's right arm without seeking glory or prestige for themselves. Engineers must recognize this. To complicate the issue further, top management is frequently completely oblivious to the adversary relationship between supervisors and the industrial engineer.

In some instances companies have found it expedient to deliberately overstaff their industrial engineering department and use it as a training ground to strengthen their supervisory force. At first glance this may appear to be somewhat costly. However, many progressive organizations feel that the investment is justified. What better way can a potential supervisor learn company policy and operational procedures? This practice also gives management the opportunity to observe and appraise the ability of potential supervisors to gain the acceptance of others before they are vested with the official authority to do so. Finally, it teaches prospective supervisors the need for empathy between staff industrial engineering and supervision.

Benefits of Work Measurement and Incentive Performance

Two case studies, selected at random from my files, serve to illustrate the tremendous benefits that can be acquired by a systematic approach to the principles of work measurement and incentive performance.

Case Study: Raise Wages and Salaries— Save $200,000

The Problem: This multi-plant southern textile firm utilized a classical piecework plan for the hourly employees and had for more than 17 years operated with a limited-scale incentive plan for salaried personnel. The salaried plan became inadequate because of economic changes, operational improvements, and developments within the company's facilities and organization. Supervisory base salaries needed to be updated to meet community norms, and their capabilities required redefinition in terms of present and future needs. Labor turnover was over 100% annually, and the company hired and trained hundreds of new employees each year. Absenteeism was significantly high for the six-days-a-week, round-the-clock operation.

Corrective Action Taken: The basic objective was to develop an incentive plan that would establish new initiatives, reward the supervisors commensurate with their performance, and promote a sense of urgency to control costs within the organization.

Eight weighted cost-improvement factors were incorporated in the plan to optimize the utilization of plant facilities, production equipment, and human resources. Specific factors to improve quality, reduce absenteeism, control labor turnover, maintain plant safety, and measure performance against indirect materials and supply budgets were also designed into the plan. The plan assured management a ratio of at least a five-to-one return (cost reduction to incentive).

The supervisory plan took hold almost immediately, and the plant workers' interest began to surface regarding the new concept. The company responded and expanded the incentive opportunity to cover hourly direct- and indirect-labor employees. An incentive plan was developed similar to the framework of the supervisory plan, except that only the factors of equipment utilization, quality, and safety were considered because this incentive pay would be additional to individual piece-rate or hourly base earnings.

The theory behind the new plantwide approach, or group incentive plan, was to encourage a more consistent overall operating performance and create improvements in quality, production, and materials. The company management believed that compensation tied to a group effort would encourage a teamwork approach and everyone would benefit.

Results Effected: Supervision, provided with a new management tool, had a new awareness, and a conscientious effort emerged in every phase of the operation. Productivity improvements reduced costs beyond projections despite the wage increases. The company was now paying its production supervisors, support personnel, and hourly employees top salaries and wages in the community.

Major cost and operational advantages were easily pinpointed and included tangible cost reductions of $200,000 annually. Labor performance increased 7% over the previous two years, and critical equipment utilization was 95%, an improvement of 5% to 7%. Absenteeism was reduced by 50%, and labor turnover leveled off at 27%, the lowest in the company's history. And the average incentive yield from the new plan paid the hourly worker an additional 17%.

Case Study: Cut Costs and Increase Production

The Problem: This eastern manufacturer of automotive and aircraft tires abandoned its wage incentive program after having tried it for an extended period. The old incentive system was finally discarded when it became obvious that through neglect it had gotten out of control and was creating havoc with the profit and loss statement. Following an all too familiar pattern, the company operated for some time thereafter on a measured day-work plan, expecting to get incentive performance for a flat hourly rate, with even more disappointing results.

The company could not afford the massive investment required for new, less labor-intensive equipment. Better utilization of existing equipment and manpower was needed. The industrial engineering function had been weakened through personnel changes. Performance rating procedures had been allowed to change in an evolutionary manner, and the calculation of various allowances had been pyramided. Mechanical delays, out-of-stock conditions, and other production problems often went unreported. Productivity targets were theoretically designed to get an incentive performance; however, only a rare individual will consistently work at a 125% performance level when the worker's pay is the same regardless of the effort.

Corrective Action Taken: Analysis determined that the incentive plan that failed was poorly conceived in the first place. The manufacturing staff lacked the level of competence and training needed when they embarked on the program. And they did not take the time required to properly engineer and install rules for the program's maintenance that would insure its survival. It was apparent that an intensive program of reindoctrination and training was needed, and it had to include first-line supervisors as well as union representatives and the workers themselves. A program to train both management and the union in the principles and techniques of work measurement was established. Some of the more common abuses, such as rate cutting and other inequities, were frankly and openly discussed.

An incentive manual containing the fundamental parts of a good incentive program was drafted. It was presented to the union and received its blessing. A provision was made for periodic audits of work standards to correct the deadly creeping changes that generally occur in an incentive program. Included as management policy was the assurance that it would do whatever possible to maintain the incentive earnings opportunity by minimizing production downtime and delays. The contract provided the union with a direct channel of communication to openly discuss any fears or concerns.

Since it is a foregone conclusion that wage incentives can never be a substitute for sound supervision and a well-trained industrial engineering department—the basic ingredients for success in any incentive program—a great deal of emphasis was placed on the critical role of these two groups.

Once the preparatory work of training, organizing, and negotiating was completed, the last step was implementation—the final acid test. At this stage there were commitments to specific courses of action, schedules, and due dates. Management expected improvements in productivity, and the employees were anxious to take home more pay. The pressure was on!

Results Effected: The incentive standards were installed, and program coverage was in effect on about 95% of direct labor operations. Straight-time average hourly earnings went up 20.1%, and productivity per man-hour increased 23.4%. Total units and weight into the warehouse increased proportionately. Production downtime was reduced significantly, and machine utilization improved because of concerted efforts to improve operations. This was a situation where there were no losers. Employee earnings were competitive in the community again at the same time that operating costs improved. Management regained its credibility with the union because the program was working as planned.

four

Indirect Labor Can Be Controlled

I keep six honest serving men;
(They taught me all I knew)
Their names are What and Why and When
And How and Where and Who.

Rudyard Kipling, "The Elephant's Child"

During the past decade, huge strides have been made in the measurement and control of direct labor. According to the Department of Labor, direct labor jobs have decreased by 9.5% during the last 10 years. From the productivity standpoint, that's good news. The bad news is that during this same period indirect labor and service functions have increased by a staggering 54.7%! White-collar and service employment combined are projected to be 2.5 times that of the blue-collar workforce. That's approximately 72% of the nation's entire workforce!

The information contained in this chapter is taken with permission from my manual, *Indirect Labor Measurement and Control,* Copyright 1980 American Institute of Industrial Engineers, 25 Technology Park/Atlanta, Norcross, GA 30092.

Bad as they are, these statistics should not really shock anyone. What else could be expected when controls in the indirect labor areas are virtually nonexistent and management tends to regard many indirect labor activities as an uncontrollable Frankenstein or simply "the cost of doing business"?

Among those companies that do attempt to employ controls on indirect labor, 43% do so by the simple expedient of adjusting indirect labor costs at a fixed percentage of those used on production activities. From a practical standpoint this is roughly analogous to basing a company's power and light bill on the number of employees on the payroll.

Target for Cost Reduction

In the factory, high indirect labor skills such as maintenance, tool and die, production setup, and other comparable technically skilled job functions are often poorly utilized because of no work measurement or labor control. In the office, clerical employees are added rather indiscriminately to offset peak workloads—not on the basis of engineered standards or measured workloads. Furthermore, in many industries the indirect labor hourly wage rates are rapidly approaching or exceeding those of direct labor, yet there is a widespread disparity in productive output between the two groups.

The situation is being even further aggravated because many wage packages being developed today call for greater fringe benefits. Fringe packages run from 30% to 60% of the total compensation cost, depending on contractual agreements or wage and salary policies applied. In other words, an employee making $12,000 a year is actually costing the company between $15,600 and $19,200, depending on the percentage of fringe benefits applied. And if the 50% productivity factor is considered when measuring real output, the actual wage cost is over $31,200 per year. The magnitude of this figure and the projected indirect growth rate make it mandatory that indirect labor costs be controlled.

Applied Measurement

A broad range of work measurement techniques are available to control indirect labor—the chief ones being direct observations, work sampling, time study, and job estimates. The applicability of the different measurement techniques can be described graphically. At one end of the spectrum is the well-defined, highly repetitive type of job similar in nature to direct labor. At the other end is the vaguely identified, long-cycle work, often involving less motion but more mental effort. An order picker or file clerk is an example of someone in a repetitive job, while positions such as a computer programmer or design engineer describe the more complex work. A detailed work study would be more practical for the repetitive jobs, while project estimates would suffice for the others.

Many indirect jobs, for example, have cycle times that range from minutes to hours and even days, depending on the type of work performed. Their methods, being less repetitive and predictable, involve more creativity, more mental processes and problem-solving ability than their direct labor counterpart.

For these basic reasons, standards of performance for indirect operations need not be as absolute or precise as those established for direct labor. They should, however, be representative of the workload requirements and serve as a management tool for planning and controlling the individual and group work effort as well.

The key to measuring tasks in indirect labor areas is maintaining consistency in the application of the measurement technique, not in setting precise or exact standards of measurement.

Major Benefits

The major benefits of a planned approach to an indirect labor measurement and control program are higher worker productivity, lower payroll and unit costs, and better management practices.

1. *Productivity improvements.* Questions arise in the executive chambers regarding how much can be gained by measuring the indirect labor employee, the size of the savings, and whether it is wise or practical to undertake such a program. In my experience, approximately 75% of the clerical, administrative, and factory support departments can be included in a measurement and control program. Typical areas include general office, technical, and administrative functions, warehousing, maintenance, and manufacturing services.

By developing a program for measurement of indirect labor, cost reductions of 15% to 30% can be realized, and the return on investment will be paid back three to five times over. The cost of administering the program will range from 1% to 5% of the indirect payroll.

2. *Cost reduction.* Without appropriate work measurement and labor controls, the performance of the indirect labor worker has been identified at 50% to 60% of a fair day's work, or approximately one-half what it should be. However, with a program incorporating measurement and controls developed for the operation, labor performance can be increased to 75%, even 90%. The improvement factor in indirect labor utilization will generally represent more than a 20% reduction in payroll costs. At today's prices, that's not a bad investment.

3. *Management practices.* Although lower payroll cost is the principal benefit to be realized, management gets many other advantages by adopting an indirect labor control program. Such a program often involves:

- Improving the productivity climate within the organization.
- Utilizing better operating procedures and work-related methods.
- Simplifying the work content into manageable units.
- Establishing standards of performance at all levels.
- Using modern techniques of work planning and job scheduling.

- Developing appropriate management controls.
- Reemphasizing the work ethic and a sense of urgency.

All this adds up to better planning and control of indirect labor hours.

Establishing Management Control

The necessity for establishing management operating control through appropriate work measurement can best be exemplified by Parkinson's Law, "Work expands to fill the time available for completion," and its corollary, "Employees multiply at a fixed rate regardless of the quantity of work they produce." Less than one-third of industrial firms and corporate offices effectively control their indirect labor costs. However, before corrective action can be effectively applied, one fundamental concept must be considered in attempting to control the indirect labor force. That is, unless the front-line supervisor is held accountable for controlling costs, any soundly engineered and well-designed cost reduction program will become virtually worthless.

The concept that cost control begins with the supervisor, as it relates to productivity management, means that any effective system of hands-on control must incorporate accountability guidelines from the time the supervisor initially assigns work to the employees, to the time the jobs in the department are satisfactorily completed.

In addition to the concept of supervisory accountability, another essential program factor must be presented. That is, executive management must make an earnest but direct commitment regarding the intent to implement a cost reduction program. This must be a highly visible commitment in the organization and not just a passive gesture if the program is to be viable.

After the program has been fully implemented, the supervisor must be charged with the responsibility of maintaining cost control in the department, and his or her performance should be measured against predetermined accountability benchmarks.

Increasing Productivity of the Service Worker

Controlling the burgeoning cost trends in indirect labor payrolls and increasing the productivity of the service worker are major challenges confronting management today. Research studies of clerical and administrative employees—the largest element of the white-collar workforce—indicate that unparalleled opportunities await management's initiative with regard to generating work improvements and cost reductions in the office. And what is most alarming, these opportunities for improving bottom-line results largely go unnoticed.

Employment trends over the past two decades indicate a dramatic rise in the white-collar workforce, with a greater increase projected for the 1980s. The principal concentration of clerical and administrative employment is in the banking, finance, insurance, and medical and health-care industries. Manufacturers, too, are very heavily involved in the service field.

Reasons for these trends are numerous—consumer demand, competition, maintaining more specialized types of customer service, and the proliferation of paperwork and record-keeping requirements because of governmental regulations. However, despite this white-collar employment explosion, management has been focusing its attention primarily on improving direct labor operations in the factory. My experience indicates that companies expend around 80% of their productive effort to control about 20% of the real labor cost. The collective effort of industrial engineering and other company personnel must be more productively deployed elsewhere in the organizaion.

Considering that the present trend in white-collar and service-worker employment will continue, management must be concerned about the decline of corporate profits and the deterioration of company service unless appropriate corrective action is taken at all levels of the organization. The indirect labor program helps provide the answer.

Basic Approach to Labor Control

A partial solution to this management dilemma has evolved from our research and job-related experience with the service worker. My associates and I devised a three-dimensional program to effect productivity improvement and cost control in clerical and manufacturing support operations. The principal elements of the program focus on:

- Appropriate training and indoctrination of the workforce, supervision, and management.
- Basic systems analysis of work flow, procedures, and operating improvements.
- Applied work measurement for manpower planning and operating control.

Realizing any appreciable gains in productivity improvements requires integrating these three elements with a program for management controls and labor reporting and a continuing effort at improvement. Let us look at each of these aspects of control.

1. *Program training.* Work analysts selected for the project should be thoroughly trained in all facets of indirect labor measurement and control so that they can be adept in counseling supervisors and managers when necessary in developing and implementing the program.

Supervisors should be oriented in principles of work measurement, labor controls, and the overall application of the program. They must understand the concepts and participate in the design and development of the cost avoidance program at the outset if it is to be successful. The workers should also be briefed by their supervisor in program fundamentals related to their jobs.

Managers must be indoctrinated in how the program

works. A working grasp of the program mechanics is essential if managers are to be held accountable for affecting cost savings in their areas of responsibility. Most of the successful programs are launched through a collective team effort and a genuine commitment from middle and upper management.

2. *Work identification and basic systems analysis.* An operations analysis, which is basically a preliminary study, should be made of the facility or operation to be improved. The study determines the current rate of labor productivity and the state of operating effectiveness. It uncovers marginal areas that may require corrective action improvements even before any indirect labor program is implemented. The checklist of twenty questions (Figure 1) may be used as a reference base in conducting the operations analysis. It will provide a general appraisal of the facility's operating condition.

The next step is to review the major work activities performed by the employees in the department. Examples of major tasks are:

Activity	Unit
Process invoice	Invoice
Type document	Document
Deliver parts	Trip
Repair machine	Work order
Process shop order	Shop order

This identification of key work activities is important because they function as major indicators and are used as tools to forecast manpower requirements and to adjust levels of staffing to meet business requirements.

The analysis of these tasks provides management with a basis to simplify and methodize the work. Work improvements are very important to the program. By making basic improvements in operating procedures, equipment, and work station layout—and not just concentrating on developing work measurement applications—management will

Figure 1. Checklist of twenty questions on productivity.

How Productive Is Your Company?

	Yes	No
1. Are late starts, early quits, and excessive personal and coffee break times controlled effectively?	____	____
2. Is management utilizing balanced crewing conditions to improve output and reduce man-hours?	____	____
3. Is the flexibility of employees adequate for performing other jobs within the department?	____	____
4. Are time-reporting forms and procedures designed to establish a sufficient basis for labor control?	____	____
5. Does management exercise control over idle and nonproduction time in the department?	____	____
6. Are job assignments batched or grouped to reduce delays and increase productivity?	____	____
7. Are the work methods and work station layouts currently being utilized practical and efficient?	____	____
8. Does management measure employee output against a predetermined norm?	____	____
9. Are manpower requirements correlated to measure output?	____	____
10. Are work assignments planned to offset fluctuations in materials and equipment availability?	____	____
11. Are attempts being made to minimize work duplications or overlapping of work assignments?	____	____

Figure 1. (continued)

12. Are peaks and valleys in workload controlled to minimize the necessity of adding manpower or working overtime? ＿＿ ＿＿

13. Does management exercise control over employee turnover in the department? ＿＿ ＿＿

14. Are the number of job classifications and the ratio of job classes to employees excessive? ＿＿ ＿＿

15. Is management utilizing historical data as a guide in determining staffing needs? ＿＿ ＿＿

16. Does the supervisor investigate chronic absenteeism? ＿＿ ＿＿

17. Do the employees receive adequate instruction and training on how to do their jobs more efficiently? ＿＿ ＿＿

18. Do the supervisors understand their role as productivity managers in the organization? ＿＿ ＿＿

19. Is the labor force adjusted to correspond with changes in business volume? ＿＿ ＿＿

20. Have there been any appreciable operational changes introduced regarding equipment, layout, or business forms in the past 3 to 5 years? ＿＿ ＿＿

strengthen its credibility and will better enlist the workers' help to improve operations and control costs.

3. *Work measurement techniques.* Work input data derived from the major tasks performed in the department have now been accumulated and analyzed. The findings will be used in developing work measurement and determining the proper staffing levels for the department.

The appropriate measurement technique should be selected and utilized accordingly when making the indirect labor studies. Various work measurement techniques are available, of which the less complicated are generally the best because "precise" standards are not usually necessary. The cost of standards maintenance must also be considered; more precision usually means more maintenance.

The most common work measurement techniques are direct observations, work sampling, and time study. Standard data can be developed from any of these, and more than one form of measurement can be used in the productivity program. The chief benefit of work measurement is the feedback. Supervision and management are provided with accurate and timely report data highlighting worker productivity, time spent on measured work, and cost effectiveness.

When work output standards have been developed for the various activities in the department or work center, workloads should be balanced and evenly distributed among the employees where practical. The staffing requirements can now be more reliably determined, and adjustments in manpower can be made accordingly before implementing the program. This is accomplished by making a manpower analysis of the department under study. The manload is calculated from volume data collected for a period representing approximately one month and from measurement standards developed for the key activities. (The output of the department may be expressed on a weekly basis for planning purposes.)

Here are data representing the major work activity of a typical department:

Activity:　Processing invoices
Standard:　6 minutes (.10 hour) per invoice
Units produced per week:　1,810 invoices
Hours required per week;　181 measured hours
Present staffing:　8 employees

Using these data, the proper manload for the department can be determined as follows:

$$\text{Units produced} \times \text{Unit Standard} = \text{Hours required}$$
$$1810 \quad \times \quad .10 \quad = \quad 181$$

$$\text{Net hours available*} - \text{Hours required} = \text{Excess hours}$$
$$304 \quad - \quad 181 \quad = \quad 123$$

$$\frac{\text{Weekly excess hours}}{\text{Hours in work week}} = \text{Equivalent excess employees}$$

$$\frac{123}{40} = 3.1$$

Staffing guides should be established at variable work input volumes to maintain proper crewing levels. These guides, or charts, show the relationship of business volume and staffing required to process the workload in the department.

The framework for constructing a staffing guide using data developed for a representative department is as follows:

Major volume indicator: Invoices processed
Minutes per invoice: 6 (.10 hours)
Hours available weekly per employee: 40
Units processed per man-week: 400 (40 divided by .10)

The staffing guide shown in Figure 2, based on these data, expresses staffing requirements in increments of .5 employees because it enables management to work overtime to handle brief increases in volume, rather than add another employee. Temporary help can also be considered in this situation.

4. *Management control and labor reporting.* After the work measurement phase of the project is completed, labor controls should be developed. Labor controls are the principal management tools used to contain costs.

Management should install a manpower utilization re-

*Calculated by subtracting estimated absenteeism, vacations, and so on from total hours available; in this case, 320 − 16 = 304.

Figure 2. Typical staffing chart.

Accounts Payable Department Weekly Staffing Chart	
Invoices Processed	*Required Staffing*
1–400	1.0
401–600	1.5
601–800	2.0
801–1000	2.5
1001–1200	3.0
1201–1400	3.5
1401–1600	4.0
1601–1800	4.5
1801–2000	5.0

porting system to monitor employee activity and evaluate individual and departmental performance. This reporting system is an integral part of the total program and is a useful accountability tool that extends from the worker to the supervisor and further up to the manager. A manual of operating procedures is then prepared to assure maintenance of the program as it is installed.

Upon completion of the productivity study, management makes a pre-installation check to point out any sensitive areas of employee concern. It will identify work flow problems that have not been improved and highlight conditions requiring corrective action before the actual installation of the program.

The major factors in making the program work as designed are numerous and revolve around the supervisor. The key actions that supervision and management must be concerned with are listed below.

- Determine the required staff level *before* installing the program and maintain balanced staffing in the department.

- Plan flexible workloads for assigning work to the employees. Measure progress and determine the overall workload status in the department.
- Follow up on late assignments and take corrective action to alleviate delays.
- Use the control forms as designed and follow the operating procedures in installing the program.
- Analyze manpower utilization and look for trends in input-output relationships. Monitor the workload conditions closely.
- Maintain open communications. Discuss technical and human relations problems with the appropriate people and chart a course of corrective action.
- Plan for tomorrow when developing work assignments and maintain management control over the department.

Management should also utilize the key indicators established for each area under control as barometers to forecast the planned manpower requirements at various levels of business volume. Periodic management follow-up should be routine throughout the program's development and implementation.

Examples of the basic control forms used to measure departmental and facility performance are shown in Figures 3 and 4 later in this chapter. These forms cover a manufacturing support installation but could reflect a clerical operation as well. These forms show the relationship of activities performed, standards of measurement, and labor performance. The management report is the key control document used in the productivity improvement program.

5. *Improvements to the system.* Management should establish benchmarks at the outset of the productivity program and document the possible improvements that were identified in the operations analysis. Key project responsibilities should be delegated and a timetable established to initiate further improvements to the program.

These benchmarks function as reference points to control all activities concerning the indirect labor project. A

Gantt-type activity chart is used to time-scale the job schedule and monitor planned activities in comparison to the actual events to determine project status.

Improvements to the indirect labor system can cover many facets and affect all levels of the organization. The principal improvements will come from establishing new operating procedures, adopting new business systems, utilizing better methods to process documents and related paperwork, balanced staffing, and work station redesign.

Program Results

The implementation of a productivity management program enables the progressive firm to reduce operating costs from 15% to 30%. It instills a management philosophy that costs *will* be controlled and generates a sense of urgency extending from the top of the organizational ladder down to the bottom rung.

The program recognizes the effort of the exceptional employee as well as the contribution of the everyday worker. Furthermore, studies have proven that the morale of the workforce will be improved. Management is thus provided with hands-on tools to achieve and maintain total operating control and utilize the workforce more effectively.

Application of Work Improvement Programs

The application of a work improvement program, where supervisory training, basic systems analysis, work standards, and management control are intelligently blended together, results in an effective payroll/cost control program. The program provides supervision and management with modern cost-effective tools to plan and measure workloads, improve employee productivity, and control payroll costs.

Clerical, administrative, and manufacturing support areas where work improvement programs have been effectively installed include:

- Accounting—accounts receivable and payable, credit and collections, and payroll.
- General office—purchasing, customer service, sales and billing, key punch and data processing, and order processing.
- Office services—stenography, typing, filing, printing, duplicating, and mail room.
- Technical services—drafting, engineering, cost estimating, and designing.
- Manufacturing support services—shipping and receiving, warehousing, and stockrooms.

Maintenance Cost Control

The control of maintenance operations has become an increasingly important item in the manufacturing cost structure. The cost of production interruptions related to ineffective maintenance procedures and poor control of the workforce is sizable. Although management makes many attempts to improve productivity of the maintenance workforce, it often overlooks the cost importance of maintaining plant equipment at a serviceable level.

Plant Engineering in its article "The Sad State of Maintenance Management" reported some alarming facts about maintenance management in 1975.

- In 62% of the cases analyzed, management did not know the productivity of its maintenance labor force.
- On the average, total maintenance costs were 180% of the 1970 level.
- Only 38% of maintenance superintendents were satisfied with their work-order system, the prime requisite for maintenance control.
- 55% of companies did not use work standards even for measuring repetitive maintenance tasks.
- 77% of companies did not break down maintenance craft time on work orders before assigning work.

- 62% of maintenance managers were not satisfied with their present preventive maintenance programs.

In another instance, a survey appearing in February 1974 in the AMA bulletin *Management in Practice,* conducted by a national consulting firm, found that the productivity of most maintenance operations is around 35% of what it could be. The survey, conducted at 35 large to medium-size manufacturing plants in 12 industries, found that plant workers spend only 2.6 hours of every eight-hour day working productively. The major items contributing to lost productivity were job-related activities covering handling and transporting materials and tools, idle and excessive personal time, waiting for work and receiving job instructions, and late starts and early quits.

The article went on to state that the lost productivity expressed in dollars could amount to over \$800,000 for a typical plant with 100 maintenance workers. From a practical standpoint it was pointed out that not all of those cost savings could be captured because of various factors. Nevertheless it must be emphasized that the loss could be reduced by 20% to 40% with the design and implementation of a well-structured maintenance cost control system.

It is essential for management to recognize that indirect costs *can* be controlled and to step up its efforts in that regard to get more effective maintenance at less expense. Better control over maintenance operations must be exercised, and expenditures must be reduced, if any appreciable cost improvement is to be made.

Maintenance Operations Analysis

An in-depth operations analysis of the maintenance department will determine the feasibility of developing a comprehensive maintenance management program. A detailed operational study will highlight symptoms of excessive costs, poor planning and control, operating ineffectiveness, and lack of appropriate management reporting information. Upon completion, the study will provide management with a framework for developing a maintenance cost control system that can be successfully tailored to company operations.

An analysis of the maintenance functions should cover these four categories.

1. *Organization.* Review and evaluate the principal functions of the maintenance department for organizational and operating effectiveness. The size of the maintenance operation should be objectively determined. It may be somewhat proportional to the number of production employees, but equipment attention, service levels, and the complexity of the facility's operation must also be considered in determining its proper size. The purpose of the maintenance organization and its reporting relationships and responsibilities must be clearly defined to prevent line and staff conflicts between production and maintenance.

2. *Operating effectiveness.* Analyze the cost effectiveness of the maintenance operation and look for trends in labor utilization and materials expenditures. Determine the extent that the maintenance costs are increasing by expressing this expense as a percentage of the total manufacturing cost over a three- to five-year period.

Summarize the amount of maintenance overtime worked and ascertain whether it is excessive. Review the types and frequency of cost controls used in the operation and analyze downtime records, production breakdowns, types of equipment repairs, and other factors. Determine the ratio of productive time and nonproductive time worked by craft workers and/or technicians.

Evaluate the investment in materials stores inventory and determine the availability and need for equipment replacement parts and maintenance supplies. Review the methods employed to control these materials and their replenishment and evaluate the effectiveness of the methods.

Review the general maintenance expenditures for outside services and justify these costs. Conduct work studies and make a sufficient number of observations to determine present levels of productivity and labor efficiency. Determine the flexibility of maintenance craft personnel and review the present methods of in-house training.

3. *Management planning and control.* Evaluate the methods and procedures used by supervision for planning and scheduling work assignments. Look for examples of poor conformance to work schedules and job priorities. Observe the maintenance workforce and determine how well the workers are being utilized on productive work. Ascertain the number of job delays due to parts and materials shortages and poor maintenance inventory planning.

Determine the size of the workloads in the department and evaluate the backlog condition. Compare this condition to overtime worked in the department. Analyze the frequency of man-hours assigned to correct emergency work conditions, and determine the amount of time that production equipment is down. Make a random sampling of the completed work orders and note the range in time for doing comparable jobs.

4. *Management information reporting problems.* Study the types of operational reports generated from this department and evaluate the flow of management information. Determine if the computer is used effectively in accumulating historical data and reporting maintenance information. The management information reporting function should cover activities embracing labor productivity, equipment repair costs, preventive maintenance applications, materials inventory, and workloads.

Maintenance Program Factors

As evidenced by the recent trends in maintenance costs, the need to control maintenance expenditures is more important than ever. Nine major factors to be considered in developing a viable maintenance cost control system to improve labor productivity and reduce operating expenditures are described below. The integration of these major factors will provide an effective maintenance cost control system.

1. *Maintenance training.* The training of maintenance

craft personnel and supervisors in the latest techniques, practices, and materials is an ongoing factor if a maintenance organization is to be effective. Training strengthens an organization, provides incentives to the craft workers for upgrading their skills, and creates job satisfaction.

2. *Maintenance organization.* An efficient maintenance operation begins with effective organization. The maintenance department's functions and responsibilities must be clearly defined and its relationship to the total organization must be set out accordingly. The maintenance department must be oriented to cost control and production.

The size and complexity of a maintenance operation will vary according to production requirements. Sophisticated equipment generally means that more maintenance craft specialists are required. The number of shifts operated and the location of production operations are critical factors that must be considered when estimating supervisory coverage and maintenance effectiveness.

3. *Management Controls.* Optimum control of maintenance expenditures requires a coordinated application of labor and materials controls. The work order and materials requisition are the key control documents in the maintenance cost control system.

Maintenance repair operations should be covered by a work order or job ticket. Materials or parts must be requisitioned through production cribs and charged off appropriately to the project if any semblance of cost control over materials is to be maintained.

4. *Preventive maintenance.* A viable preventive maintenance program is an integral part of a balanced maintenance cost control system. Scheduled maintenance covering systematic inspections, repairs, service, and lubrication will reduce production downtime and help control maintenance costs.

A complete preventive maintenance program should also provide for planned and scheduled replacement of troublesome production machinery and other plant equipment in the coming year.

5. *Materials inventory.* Hands-on control over maintenance materials is essential to eliminate unnecessary inven-

tory investment and reduce parts shortages. The materials requisition mentioned in item 3 above provides the basis for compiling and allocating materials costs.

Materials inventory can be controlled in a number of ways depending on the degree of management involvement desired. A manual card system using minimum and maximum levels is one method; another revolves around a computerized program of materials requirements based on historical usage.

6. *Maintenance planning and scheduling.* Optimum utilization of the maintenance workforce begins with planning and scheduling work assignments. Job priorities and maintenance workloads must be considered by the supervisor or work planner when this phase of the program is initiated. The realization of cost savings is a direct result of careful planning and scheduling of maintenance man-hours.

Using the work standards developed for the maintenance tasks, the supervisor can determine how long each job should take. The supervisor or work planner can batch the number of job tickets or maintenance requests that can be done in an eight-hour day by each craft worker.

Work assignments for each employee should be planned and generally grouped to cover an eight-hour day. This minimizes the gap between assignments and utilizes the maintenance worker more effectively. Periodic supervisory follow-up will enable the status of the work to be determined and will create a sense of urgency on the employee's part to do the job on time. Causes of delays or jobs behind schedule can also be readily determined during the follow-up process.

The basic objectives of planning and scheduling maintenance operations are:

- To plan a full day's work in advance for each craft worker so as to minimize lost time and improve labor utilization.
- To reduce backlog conditions and workloads in the maintenance department.
- To initiate better control over the maintenance labor dollar, and to handle job priorities and emergency situations more effectively.

- To improve the production process by having the machinery and equipment operating more efficiently.

Maintenance planning and scheduling are essential elements of an effective maintenance organization. They operate hand in hand in determining a full day's work for each maintenance worker.

7. *Applied work measurement.* The measurement standard is the basis for establishing manpower requirements, determining workloads, and scheduling maintenance activities. This tool is an important factor in measuring labor performance and establishing crewing levels at various inputs of work volume.

Work standards can be developed for maintenance operations using a variety of techniques. Job estimates and work sampling are most often used in developing work standards for general maintenance activities because of the number of variables involved. Job estimates can be refined to the point where they are quite accurate by using a regression analysis, which involves plotting the actual and estimated time values for each maintenance activity on a scatter diagram. Job data are synthesized into manageable time units, and realistic standard time data may be developed from the actual estimated values plotted.

Most preventive maintenance work is repetitive and can be measured; in fact, work measurement can be successfully applied to over 90% of the preventive maintenance labor hours expended. The two principal techniques for preventive maintenance are time study and predetermined times.

Work sampling is used to accumulate operations data covering equipment and machinery utilization, labor productivity, and types of production delays.

8. *Operating methods.* An effective organization needs uniform maintenance operations. This requires establishing standardized methods, working guidelines, and operational procedures. Standard operating procedures are critical to the maintenance organization. In essence, they enable maintenance workers like production operators to do a better job if they know:

What must be done.

Where the job is located.

When the job must be done.

How long the assignment should take.

What tools are required to perform the job.

What processes or steps are involved in doing the work.

The maintenance supervisor should be certain that all policies and procedures are written and followed, and that the necessary forms, paperwork, and operational guidelines are available to the worker. Trouble-shooting manuals are very important in this regard.

9. *Management reporting system.* Management reports serve as a barometer of operating effectiveness. They are used to report current progress and determine whether any corrective action is required. The reporting system is essentially a principle of management by exception and is commonly referred to as a Polaroid snapshot of an operation. That is, it will tell you what is going on in the organization— good or bad.

The principal function of the management report shown in Figure 3 is to highlight those exceptions. The report should not be used as a corrective action device; that is management's job.

Management reports are the heart of the maintenance operation and perhaps the most significant aspect of the cost reduction program.

A schematic diagram of the management information flow required in a maintenance cost control system is shown in Figure 4. This diagram covers the control process from the time the work request is generated until completion.

Case Study: Control Maintenance and Other Costs

The Problem: A midwestern auto parts manufacturer employing over 300 hourly workers saw its unit costs spiraling out of control and its market position threatened. The company had a sizable investment in capital equipment, but some

Figure 3. Report for highlighting exceptions.

REA REPORTED Indirect Labor   WEEK ENDED _____

NO.	AREA	SHIFT	STAFFING AUTH.	STAFFING ACT.	STAFFING VAR.	MVI (UNITS)	BACK-LOG HOURS AVAIL	EARNED HOURS	HOURS ON MEAS.	NON-MEAS. HOURS	FIXED HOURS	TOTAL HOURS WORKED	% PROD	% UTIL	% PERF
10	Production Stores	1	5.5	5.9	.4	110	—	163.0	212.4	21.6	-0-	234.0	77	91	70
		2	2.0	1.9	(.1)	36	—	54.5	68.5	9.5	-0-	78.0	80	88	70
		TL	7.5	7.8	.3	146	—	217.5	280.9	31.1	-0-	312.0	72	90	70
20	Shipping	1	8.0	9.8	.3	6315	644	318.5	375.0	6.0	11.0	392.0	85	96	81
		2	—	—	—	—	—	—	—	—	—	—	—	—	—
		TL	9.5	9.8	.3	6315	644	318.5	375.0	6.0	11.0	392.0	85	96	81
30	Quality Control	1	6.0	6.3	.3	360	—	181.4	218.6	15.4	16.0	250.0	82	87	73
		2	3.5	4.0	.5	245	—	123.9	153.5	6.5	-0-	160.0	81	96	77
		TL	9.5	10.3	.8	605	—	305.3	372.1	21.9	16.0	410.0	82	91	74
40	Set-up	1	5.5	6.0	.5	42	—	170.3	238.0	-0-	-0-	238.0	72	100	72
		2	2.0	2.1	.1	14	—	58.2	63.4	14.6	4.0	82.0	92	77	71
		TL	7.5	8.1	.6	56	106	228.5	301.4	14.6	4.0	320.0	76	94	71
50	Maintenance	1	12.0	12.8	.8	145	—	287.2	390.3	120.7	-0-	511.0	74	76	56
		2	10.0	10.1	.1	151	—	301.7	366.1	30.9	8.0	405.0	82	90	74
		TL	22.0	22.9	.9	296	2580	588.9	756.4	151.6	8.0	916.0	78	83	64
60	Tool Room	1	8.0	8.4	.4	96	—	285.6	304.0	26.0	6.0	336.0	94	90	85
		2	3.0	3.6	.6	32	—	101.2	129.0	15.0	-0-	144.0	78	90	70
		TL	11.0	12.0	1.0	128	1502	386.8	433.0	41.0	6.0	480.0	89	90	81
	TOTALS		65.5	70.9	5.3	---	---	2045.5	2518.8	266.2	45.0	2830.0	81	89	72

Figure 4. Diagram of management information flow
for maintenance cost control system.

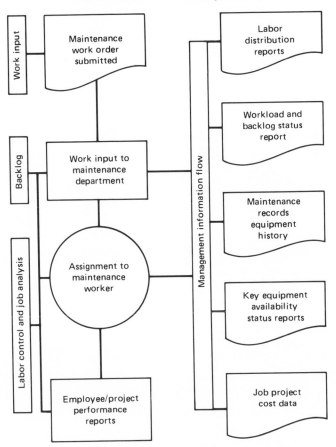

of the manual production lines outproduced the automated
ones. The key problems were production downtime, rising
indirect labor costs, too much overtime, excessive absenteeism, poor work habits, and marginal employee productivity. The indirect areas targeted for productivity improvements were maintenance and tool room, materials
handling, quality control, and warehousing.

Corrective Action Taken: The initial approach in correct-
ing the problem was to make a comprehensive operational
study of each of the major indirect areas so as to pinpoint the

high-cost labor areas and establish a program for operating improvements. Problem analysis of the direct labor areas was an integral part of the study.

Workshops were then set up to indoctrinate the plant supervisors in program concepts and the overall approach to productivity improvements. The supervisors in turn were required to present and sell the program to the bargaining employees in their areas of responsibility. The employees were apprised that work rules would be enforced and chronic absenteeism controlled. This total commitment was necessary to accomplish the objective and get the company back on track. Workers began to feel that real job security was possible, and unit costs started to go down.

A work-order system was designed and implemented in the plant maintenance area. Supervisors now had a total management control system to assign work and to monitor employee activities, to determine backlog levels and work-load requirements, to develop priorities for critical equipment, to establish crew sizes at various volume levels, and to evaluate individual and group productivity. Preventive maintenance applications and operational procedures supplemented this program.

In other indirect areas, observations were made to establish work standards. A management reporting system was installed to monitor individual productivity and departmental activity. Labor reports were generated daily and summarized weekly.

The total program as installed was designed to assess everybody's performance, from the hourly wage earner in each department under control up through supervision to management. The accountability principle applied throughout the organization.

Results Effected: Overtime was virtually eliminated in all the plant areas. Downtime was reduced, and equipment utilization went up. Indirect labor costs were slashed by a resounding 27%. Over $500,000 in cost savings was generated. The total indirect labor force was reduced by 23 employees, a reduction that enabled several skilled workers to be utilized in other key areas. Unit costs were improved considerably, and the company gained new leverage in the marketplace.

five

Upgrading the Effectiveness of Supervision

As I was going up the stair
I met a man who wasn't there.
He wasn't there again today.
I wish, I wish he'd go away.

Hughes Mearns

During the 1920s and 1930s the image of the American fore-man could be roughly described as about halfway between an army drill sergeant and an all-powerful overlord. In addition to having the right to hire, fire, promote, and transfer, the foreman of an earlier era was regarded by top management as a major motivating force in the industrial structure and was accorded a degree of prestige from both labor and man-agement. He was responsible for insuring that a maximum volume of work was performed in a fixed period of time. He was the source of technical knowledge, the leader of his worker group, and the administrator of discipline when needed. When he issued an order, the worker either re-sponded or was replaced by someone who would.

From the standpoint of management and the economy of the era, it was a good policy, simple and easy to understand. And because it worked, it is perhaps understandable how management was lulled over a period of years into the belief that things would always remain that way. Unfortunately for industry, the foreman has been the victim of change, like so many other institutions. The change has been subtle and generated by a number of factors, including proliferation of staff specialists, sophisticated mechanization, automation, cost analysis, long-range planning, time studies, and numerous other management devices that tend to usurp the foreman's former prerogatives. The result is that all too often foremen have been stripped of most of their previous authority and have in return been burdened with responsibility for a host of new duties they have had no part in developing.

Considering the heavyhanded approach used by many foremen of an earlier era, there may be some among us who derive a degree of satisfaction from the plight of today's first-line supervisor. Nevertheless, the occupational emasculation of this vital link between labor and management has, in many instances, all but wiped out many of the gains that have been acquired through improved techniques and better production methods.

Misused, Abused, and Accused

Today's foremen are the most misused, abused, and accused people in the organizational structure. They are overworked and underpaid, they have no real authority, and they must continually walk a tightrope between labor, management, and the trade unions. Foremen are subject to pressures that did not exist in prewar America. They must cope with the unprecedented power wielded by labor unions, worker's rights, and a grievance procedure under which a foreman who disciplines a worker may be called upon to defend his or her action not only to the union, but to top management as well.

Labor unions recognize this. The employees they represent know it. Indeed, the foremen themselves are acutely aware of it. The only people who seem blissfully unaware of this indisputable fact of life are the leaders of industry who pay their salaries.

Today's foremen are weighed down on all sides by cost standards, production standards, quality standards, methods, procedures, specifications, rules, regulations, laws, contracts, and agreements. Foremen survive in a sort of occupational twilight zone. Technically they are members of management, yet they are seldom invited to staff meetings and more often than not can identify more closely with the people they are being paid to supervise than with higher management. They are expected to work with staff specialists, the personnel department, industrial engineers, and accountants. They must know the union contract and how to settle grievances, how to cooperate with other department heads, how to instruct workers, how to maintain discipline, and how to cope with reams of paperwork.

The end result is that many first-line supervisors, overwhelmed by complete frustration, develop a "what's the use" attitude and ultimately relinquish the reins of leadership to workers or shop stewards. In effect they become conductors instead of motormen, and the company, in turn, suffers a predictable reduction in earnings and productivity.

Obviously, under our present industrial structure it would be impractical, and indeed undesirable, to revert to the role of the authoritarian foreman. Nevertheless, management must face up to the fact that if the present condition is to be improved, the role of the foreman must be upgraded from that of a glorified record keeper to something resembling a symbol of leadership. Management must take the initiative in this transition. Today's foremen are convinced that they are less, rather than more, effective; less, rather than more, important; less, rather than more, secure; and have received less, rather than more, recognition.

Ironically, management has played a leading role in undermining the status of the first-line supervisor. Admittedly, staff technicians, industrial engineers, quality control specialists, and cost analysis experts are a vital part of the present industrial scene. But the foreman is still the only direct link between the people who make policy and the people who perform the work. To downgrade the status of this individual either overtly or inadvertently is not only a contributing factor to poor productivity, but an insult to the initiative, intelligence, and morale of an important member of the management team.

Management must discard its current policy of treating the foreman as the "little man who wasn't there." I'll go one step further and state that the organization that has the foresight to develop and cultivate what for lack of a better term I refer to as professional foremen and pay them salaries commensurate with their abilities will reap benefits in productivity, employee morale, and increased profits many times in excess of the compensation they are required to pay for this type of expertise. To do this, management must begin by recognizing the foreman as a member of management. Many company executives claim they already do this, but for the most part their recognition consists primarily of lip service.

During a talk I gave recently to a group of company presidents, I asked for a show of hands on the question: "How many company representatives here today consider the foreman a member of management?"

The hands of nine-tenths of the audience went up.

"Now let me ask," I went on, "how many of you give your foreman an increase in pay shortly after your employees' union gets an increase following settlement of a new contract?"

The same number of hands went up.

"How can you say that you regard these foremen as members of management?" I asked. "The loyalty of these so-called members of management is tied in to your company union. They're fighting for the union to get an increase because they know perfectly well that only then will they get an increase. You gentlemen are kidding yourselves when you say you regard the foreman as a member of management!"

Adjustments to a foreman's pay should be established by

the formulas that apply to other management positions and not be dependent on results of bargaining negotiations.

Bargain-Basement Supervision—Its Cause and Effect

In a recent survey conducted by James E. Overbeke, a writer for *Industry Week,* foremen were asked how they viewed their position in military terms. Were they lieutenants (meaning officers and gentlemen) or were they sergeants (meaning straw bosses)? Every one replied: "Sergeants."

With an empathy gap like this existing between the foremen and top management, it would follow that the initial step on the part of today's industrial leaders must be first to recognize the foremen's true worth and convince them of their importance to the organization they serve. How far we are from doing this can best be illustrated by a recent advertisement that appeared in a newspaper circulated in a small American industrial city:

> WANTED: Foreman for heavy industry assembly plant. Applicant must have the ability to work with staff specialists, personnel department, industrial engineers, and maintenance staff. Must possess the ability to lead employees and stimulate their respect. Must be knowledgeable concerning the union contract, grievance procedures, work measurement, and incentive standards. Successful applicant will also be required to instruct workers, develop more effective job procedures, maintain discipline, and process paperwork generated by cost standards, production standards, quality standards, safety specifications, rules, regulations, contracts, and agreements. Salary: $16,000 a year.

Read this advertisement again. Look at the responsibilities. Then look at the salary. Does this tell us anything? It could be argued, I suppose, that the organization that placed this ad was only adhering to the law of the marketplace. The advertised pay, sad to state, is within the bounds of what is paid by many companies throughout the land. Moreover, there will be people who will be ready, and perhaps even eager, to take a job of this type at the indicated salary.

The advertised position will be filled. Make no mistake about that. But unless the organization doing the hiring is exceptionally lucky, it will be occupied by an individual who eventually, if not immediately, will lack credibility with subordinates, resent interference from staff specialists, have a low opinion of his own contribution to the organization, and harbor a marked hostility for superiors who expect him to work for wages that are probably lower than those received by the people he supervises.

Numerous studies conducted in conjunction with foreman pay structure have determined that in 60% of the companies today skilled employees take home pay equal to, or more than, their foreman. What really disturbs me is that when I point this out to managers in some of these companies, they say: "Well, Patton, look at the overtime these employees must put in to make that extra money."

My answer to this is: "The heck with the overtime. They're taking home more *money!*" I am continually amazed at how many organizations will invest millions of dollars in high-priced machinery but flatly refuse to pay for the expertise required to insure cost-effective operation of this expensive equipment.

Overlapping Lines of Authority

Not all the foreman's problems are directly linked to poor pay. Part of the difficulty can be traced to low morale generated by an overlapping of authority by staff specialists who frequently usurp the foreman's prerogatives.

The personnel director, stimulated perhaps by an ever increasing role in labor-management affairs, often either countermands or modifies a foreman's recommendation for disciplinary action with little or no explanation.

Industrial engineers and safety specialists often arbitrarily enforce changes without prior consultation with the first-line supervisor. Cost control people frequently lay out programs with only a superficial knowledge of the problems on the production line. The industrial impotence suffered by the foreman as a result of these policies results in a lowering of morale and ultimately a lack of respect for the foreman by workers, who tend to regard their immediate supervisor as an organizational nonentity with no real authority or status in the organization.

Staff personnel must be trained to channel their activities in such a manner that they work with and through the supervisors and help them increase effectiveness, instead of indulging themselves in what can only be described as a power play to control production activities.

I recall an instance that occurred when I was engaged in a plant improvement program at a southern textile mill where a departmental feud had developed between the safety officer and a foreman whom I'll refer to as Jones. Jones was a long-time employee and a production-minded supervisor who was steeped in the premise that the foreman in charge of a department should have complete license to insure maximum productivity. Predictably, when the safety officer began initiating some safety measures that impaired production, Jones tended to regard them with something less than enthusiasm.

His antagonism reached a boiling point one day when the safety man arbitrarily installed a series of machine guards in a low-risk area that created a bottleneck and affected the entire production line. The altercation that followed became loud and abusive. At the height of the argument the company president appeared on the scene, and both men were hastily summoned to the front office.

The president addressed the safety officer first. "What's the problem?" he asked.

"I've been hired here to insure the safety of the workers," the safety man replied. "Yet this man resists everything I try to accomplish."

The president turned to the foreman. "Don't you believe in safety?" he asked.

"I believe in safety as much as anyone in this plant," Jones retorted. "In 22 years of operation I've never had a lost time accident. The trouble is that our safety officer, sitting upstairs in his comfortable office, has no idea of what's needed on the production line. The necessary safety equipment was recommended and installed by me long before he came on the scene. This equipment he's putting in is unnecessary. What's worse, he doesn't even talk to me about it before it's installed."

"Do you ever discuss these matters with Mr. Jones before you implement them?" the president asked the safety officer.

"I can't talk to him!" the safety man exclaimed. "He's completely negative about any changes in the status quo."

"Would you like to receive his opinion?" the president asked.

"I'd welcome it!" the safety man retorted. "I'll readily admit Mr. Jones is more knowledgeable about his own department than I am. But so far I haven't been able to talk to him."

The problem was resolved by placing Jones as a permanent member on the safety committee, where he has since shown a marked interest in developing new and more practical safety procedures and has, in fact, contributed several valuable innovations to the safe operation of his department.

The case noted above is typical. Jones did not resent the safety measures. What he objected to was someone modifying the operation of his department without discussing the changes with him beforehand. This not only diminished his production; it also diminished his authority. And worst of all, it diminished his pride. He had pride in his supervisory judgment, which should have been respected. Once he was given an expanded role in running the operation, he was actually able to increase his contribution to the department and to the firm.

Unfortunately, in too many instances staff specialists have been a hindrance, rather than a help to the foreman who is trying to do a more effective job. We all fully realize that the complexity of modern operations demands specialized skills. However, all too often staff specialists tend to ignore the foreman as a member of the management team.

Another area of conflict involves personnel representatives who often encourage employees to bring questions and problems to the personnel department, rather than encouraging them to go to the foreman and have them handled directly by him or her. Personnel people often claim that the foreman is not capable of handling these situations. In many instances this is only an excuse to build their own bureaucracy rather than assuming responsibility for providing the education and know-how that would permit foremen to stand on their own. Such personnel people evaluate their own importance by the activity of the personnel department rather than by how helpful they can be in assisting the foreman. They have, in effect, become a self-serving entity rather than functioning as a positive supportive arm to supervision—which, in the final analysis, is an important reason for their very existence.

Industrial engineers have also in many instances done their companies a disservice by minimizing the foreman's stature in the organization. Too many industrial engineers today impose their industrial engineering methods and techniques on foremen rather than working with and through them. A giant step in improving the relationship between the industrial engineer and the first-line supervisor would be for engineers to work hard to insure that supervisors get credit for any and all accomplishments in their departments. Staff assistance should, of course, be made available, but the staff should not be given the authority to dictate to the foremen.

I'm not suggesting that these conditions exist in every organization, but they occur often enough to constitute an extremely serious problem in many companies today. I realize that I'm being quite harsh with some staff specialists who may be readers of this book, so let me temper my remarks to a degree and say that I don't blame these staff specialists too much for these actions. What I really blame is top management, which is frequently oblivious to the conditions that undermine foremen's authority and effectiveness and does nothing about them.

Communications

The dictionary defines communication as "an exchange of ideas through speech or writing." In my opinion the key word in this sentence is "exchange." From the standpoint of this definition as it applies to the industrial community, management has done a miserable job of communicating with the people who can help it the most.

In more than 30 years that I have spent in the management consulting field, I have yet to find a company where the supervisory force felt that management was doing a good job of communications. When we approach foremen on the subject of communications, we get only one answer: "Yes, they tell us what they want us to know. But that's where it stops. They never listen to us."

Management has concentrated on the downward side of communications and just about ignored the upward side of the picture. This hasn't worked. I'll go a step further and state that management's present attitude of talking down to supervision is one of the major factors in the demoralization of the American foreman.

It is vitally important that supervisors, as members of management, be kept continuously informed concerning changes in policy, organization, or conditions that affect their departments. They must receive the backing and support of higher management with reasonable speed. Yet in company after company we find that proposed changes manage to leak down to the rank and file before the first-line supervisor is even aware of them. In seven out of ten companies, union stewards know more about company policy than the foremen do. There's been too much talk about communication and too little action.

I recall an incident that occurred during a presentation I gave to one of our largest metalworking trade associations. I made the statement that in four out of five companies today, the union steward knows more about the contract than the supervisor. One of the presidents in the group took me up on this statement and said, "My supervisor has to watch production, keep costs down, watch quality, and on and on; how can he possibly know as much about the contract as the steward?" My answer to him was simply this: "Unfortunately, you are 100% right; however, take that attitude and you take the consequences. It's up to you to see that he knows."

Few companies take advantage of a supervisory newsletter, which can be mailed to a foreman's home on a confidential basis. This gives the supervisor a feeling of being privy to things that are not available to the people he or she supervises. Too many companies feel that this is too costly or too much work. My feeling is that they cannot afford *not* to, from a standpoint of either time or money.

Only about 10% of today's organizations have taken the trouble to schedule monthly dinner meetings with first-line supervision, and in a good portion of these, the communication is mostly downward, with little credence being given to input from the foremen themselves. To be effective, a meeting of this type must consist of a mutual exchange of ideas. It should also be attended by the sales manager, staff personnel, and the marketing manager.

If management is sincere about upgrading the role of the supervisor, it will be necessary to spend time to assure the foremen that they are truly part of the organizational team. This, incidentally, must be top management's *own time*. It is a commodity that cannot be delegated to someone at a relatively low rung on the administrative totem pole.

A few years ago I conducted a survey of foremen at a large midwestern utility plant. Fifty first-line supervisors were asked the question: "Why are some supervisors reluctant to exercise authority over employees under their jurisdiction?"

This was not a multiple-choice question. The participants had to think about and compose their replies. In spite of this, 36 out of the 50 foremen who were queried stated that they did not feel that they had adequate backing from top management. Warranted or not, this attitude on the part of a majority of first-line supervisors is a clear indication that something is wrong. Regardless of the reasoning behind their foremen's thinking, top management should set the record straight, either by taking a greater interest in the foremen's problems or by explaining to them the reasons for their apparent apathy.

Foreman Selection

In many instances the first-line supervisor in charge of a department is selected on the basis of qualifications that are entirely unrelated to criteria that define an effective supervisor. In four out of five companies where I served as a consultant, the foreman had been promoted to his present job because he was the best machine operator or the senior man in his department. This practice may ruffle fewer feathers, but from a standpoint of maximum effectiveness any correlation between a good producer and a capable leader is purely coincidental.

If promotional policy of this type is followed (and there are, admittedly, some practical reasons for doing this), it is simply not enough to approach a worker on a Friday evening with the statement: "Joe, starting Monday morning you're taking over the department." Occasionally management might condescend to add: "There'll also be a $10.00 a week raise in it for you." However, the person selected may not even want the added responsibility. Assuming that he or she does, any promotion of this nature that is not followed up by a vigorous training program can be an open invitation to disaster.

The importance of this cannot be emphasized too strongly. In the course of numerous foreman improvement programs in which I have participated over the years, we developed a series of questions designed to assess a foreman's strong points and shortcomings. We later expanded the program to include shop stewards, which turned up an extremely interesting development: When the same ques-

Figure 5. Compared test scores of union stewards and company foremen.

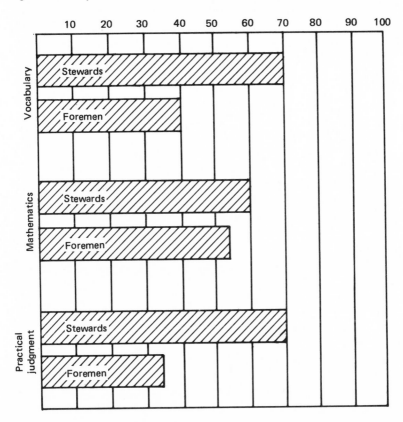

tions were given to foremen and union stewards in the 35 companies tested, the union stewards attained higher scores in such areas as mathematics, vocabulary, and practical judgment than did the foremen. (See Figure 5.)

When we first analyzed these findings, the results seemed almost incomprehensible. However, a review of the situation made it more understandable. After all, the stewards were usually selected by the democratic process for their ability to lead. On the other hand, most of the foremen were in their present position because of seniority or because they were the most productive machine operator or best assembler.

In light of these findings, is it any wonder that the shop

steward has in many instances managed to wrest the reins of leadership from the person who is being paid to run the show? Put another way: *If the foreman doesn't lead, the shop steward will.*

Proper foreman selection is a vital part of management's duties and responsibilities. During the selection process, management should consider a number of factors in addition to an employee's seniority and work record. To cite a few:

1. Make sure candidates have the leadership abilities required to make them good supervisors.
2. Be sure they want to be supervisors. Of today's foremen, 25% never wanted to be supervisors in the first place.
3. Insure them take-home pay at least 20% greater than that of the skilled people who work for them.
4. Be sure they are people-conscious and will not lose sight of the fact that they are a part of management and responsible for company objectives.
5. Be certain they have enough self-confidence to be interested in doing a job instead of winning a popularity contest with employees.
6. Be sure they have training that is appropriate for the specific job and that helps correct their own particular weaknesses.

All these factors are vital to the making of a good supervisor. To the employee, the supervisor *is management.* And as a viable member of management he or she must have the necessary equipment to insure a role of leadership.

Foreman Training

If we accept the fact that foremen today are poorly paid, poorly selected, poorly trained, and only marginally effective, it follows that a top-priority program on the part of management must be developed not only to insure better selection of future foremen but to upgrade the effectiveness of those who currently control operations.

Half a billion dollars will be spent this year on foreman training, yet it is hard to believe that management is getting its money's worth. Most foreman training programs fall short of their mark for a variety of reasons.

First of all, most foreman training programs are conducted in a classroom and consist primarily of textbook guidelines that were designed to fit a multitude of problems that have little bearing on actual shop conditions. They consist, for the most part, of canned rhetoric delivered on a "talk down" basis with little provision being made for student feedback. Additionally, these sessions are often conducted in a setting that tends to inhibit participants from contributing valuable input. To have maximum effect, a training program must be designed to fit actual shop conditions and problems as they exist on the supervisor's day-to-day job. This takes time and a little expense, but the rewards of tailoring a program to the needs of a specific organization can be tremendous.

Another shortcoming in existing foreman training programs is that all too frequently staff personnel, with whom the foreman must work, have not been included. It is essential that these people should be included, if for no other reason than to make them aware of the unique problems faced by the people on the firing line.

A major factor in the ultimate success of a training program can be enlisting the aid of some of the foremen themselves in designating the subject matter to be discussed. It is also best to make it clear before the program begins that the curriculum will consist of workshop sessions rather than stereotyped lectures.

If we are ready to admit that what America needs more than a good five-cent cigar is a good professional foreman, I can heartily recommend a program that has been developed over the years, one that has been enormously successful in upgrading the effectiveness of supervision. The program has been used in literally dozens of widely diversified industries, and in no instance has it failed to result in a marked improvement in supervisory morale and effectiveness. For lack of a better term I refer to this program as a supervisory inventory. It consists of determining the qualifications, needs, and attitudes not only of the foremen, but of top management as well.

The Supervisory Inventory

The supervisory inventory must be tailored to the specific needs of an organization, so it may vary somewhat from one company to another. Still, the guidelines listed here can be easily adapted to any organization with a little time and effort.

The first step in the inventory is the development of an anonymous questionnaire to be answered by all first-line supervisors. In circulating this questionnaire it should be emphasized that it is *not* to be signed. It should also be pointed out that the survey is not designed to determine individual weaknesses. On the contrary, it is being conducted to pinpoint weaknesses of current company programs and policies.

All questions should be of the yes-or-no type, or at least should require no elaborate answer. However, if a supervisor wishes to expand on replies, he or she should be encouraged to do so on the blank side of the page.

Although the questions asked will vary from one company to another, a typical list might consist of the following:

1. Do you understand the basis of the company's wage and salary compensation plans?
2. Do you know how our pay rates compare with those of similar jobs in our area?
3. Do you know on what basis a new job is evaluated?
4. Do you know how to check to determine if an employee is giving a fair day's work?
5. Do you keep productivity records for each employee?
6. Do you know whom to report to when standards are not met?

7. Does your department have periodic peaks and valleys in production?
8. Do you, as a supervisor, advise employees promptly when there are sudden changes in production scheduling, procedures, or working conditions?
9. Do you have problems in your department that you feel you cannot solve by yourself?
10. Do you feel that top management is sympathetic toward employees and sincerely wants you to be fair and square with them?
11. Do you make a record of the questions asked of you by employees?
12. Do you feel that the company is providing sufficient benefits?
13. Do you know what methods are used to hire the right person for the right job?
14. Are you usually consulted about hiring an employee for your own department?

These questions are not all-inclusive, but they give a fair idea of the type of information that can be obtained by means of a supervisory audit. The results of this audit will reveal the weaknesses that top management must recognize *and correct* before any meaningful improvement can be expected from first-line supervision.

Following a tabulation of the topics in greatest need of attention, an announcement should be made of a new type of supervisory program. This will consist of meetings of not more than ten to fifteen supervisors, conducted on company time, during which each of the subjects in need of attention will be discussed in the order of their importance. The person conducting these meetings should be skilled in communications, especially in use of visual aids and other training devices. Any new solutions arrived at after a thorough discussion of the items in need of resolution should be written up, placed into a binder issued to each supervisor, and thereafter recognized as the official revised policy manual.

The next step is for management to back up the findings by *action*. Top management cannot afford to complacently sit back at this point and assume that it has done its part. Management must now engage in a vigorous program of setting an example for its supervisors. It must begin by recognizing that a portion of the blame for the supervisors' shortcomings must be laid at management's doorstep.

The areas where management might be in need of improvement can be determined by a management self-audit, similar to the supervisory self-audit conducted for foremen. To accomplish this, another questionnaire should be developed and circulated among top management. Questions that might be included in this survey include:

1. Is the pay differential between your skilled workers and your supervisors sufficient?
2. Is your supervisory pay plan based on individual merit, or is it tied to other factors like a fixed amount more than the wage settlements negotiated with the employee union?
3. Are your foremen informed about changes in policy, organization, or conditions that affect their department before the same information is circulated to the rank and file?
4. Do you back up the foremen in their decisions?
5. Have you sometimes countermanded foremen's judgment summarily, without giving them a chance to explain the reason for their actions?
6. Is management more interested in the profit picture than it is in its supervisors, their needs, and their problems?
7. Does top management make a continual effort to keep in touch with the foremen's thinking?
8. Do members of top management know all their supervisors by name?
9. Do you, on occasion, usurp the foremen's prestige by dispensing information to the union and shop stewards before the foremen themselves are aware of it?
10. Have you ever made a sincere effort to tell first-line supervisors about company problems?

11. Do you publish a supervisory newsletter that is mailed to the homes of first-line supervisors?
12. Are foremen given any training prior to assuming their duties?
13. Are foremen given any training after assuming their duties?
14. If so, are these training programs geared to the foremen's actual working conditions, rather than stereotyped guidelines and canned platitudes?
15. Have you ever asked for the cooperation of first-line supervisors in solving problems that would normally be resolved by top management?
16. Have you established a supervisory incentive program by which foremen can acquire additional compensation for superior accomplishments?
17. If so, is this program geared to a cost-saving ratio rather than abstract factors like the judgment of middle or top management?
18. Have you ever engaged in a real effort to establish better rapport between foremen and the staff specialists with whom they must work?
19. Do you permit employees to bring problems to administrative support areas like the personnel department, instead of first presenting them to their immediate supervisor?
20. Have foremen received any formal training in grievance procedures or interpretation of the union contract?
21. Has any effort been made to acquaint foremen with the need for specialized units like industrial engineering, safety, and other support areas with which they must work?
22. Do you have any clear-cut program by which a foreman may be promoted to middle management?
23. Do you regard the foremen as the managers of their work areas, rather than as straw bosses carrying out only those orders and decisions passed down from higher up?
24. Do you conduct periodic performance reviews of all first-line supervisors?

25. If so, do you attempt to alleviate shortcomings that are noted as a result of these performance reviews?
26. Do you tell your foremen when they're doing a good job?
27. Do you select foremen carefully, or are they, as a general rule, promoted on the basis of being the best production worker in the department or having the most seniority?
28. Do you make any effort to determine whether supervisors are treating subordinates as individuals and with the consideration needed to earn employee respect?

These questions, if answered sincerely, will call for a large degree of soul-searching on the part of top managers. Most executives who approach this questionnaire with a positive attitude will find conditions that appear to call for some form of remedial action on their part. Human nature being what it is, some managers may even try to rationalize obvious shortcomings. But make no mistake, whether they admit to these deficiencies or not, others in the organization will know about them and wonder why nothing is being done to correct them. No doubt establishment of better rapport between supervision and higher management will call for considerable time and effort. Yet managerial inaction is a trait that executives cannot afford to possess if they expect to continue in their present positions for very long.

With a positive attitude by all parties concerned, and with a comprehensive program of supervisory training and development based on organizational needs and accompanied by appropriate follow-through by *both* supervisors and management, supervisory effectiveness *can* be attained. A word of caution, though. Top management may, by virtue of its rank, be in a position immune from serious participation and may therefore assume an attitude of inaction, or only superficial support. If this is done the program will not be effective.

It takes big human beings to recognize and remedy deficiencies in their own performance that they may be in a position to overlook. But the managers who make a sincere attempt to judge themselves by the same criteria that they apply to subordinates will be the ones who benefit most from a program of this type.

If nothing is done, the status of the American foreman will continue to be summed up by a sign that hangs over the desk of a shift foreman in a Detroit auto plant:

> They don't let me run the train;
>   the whistle I can't blow.
> I'm not allowed to work the switch,
>   or make the engine go.
> I'm not allowed to let off steam,
>   or even ring the bell.
> But let the damn thing jump the track,
>   and see who catches hell!

six

Assuring Results
Through Accountability

Pity the overworked executive! Behind his paperwork ramparts, he struggles bravely with a seemingly superhuman load of responsibilities. Burdened with impossible assignments, beset by constant emergencies, he never has a chance to get organized. Pity him—but recognize him for the dangerous liability that he is.

Clarence B. Randall

Executive accountability is the most underrated and overlooked management tool in American industry. If this sentence sounds like an overstatement, consider the fact that many organizations spend hundreds of thousands of dollars measuring the man on the bench or a $250-a-week machine operator, but they never give a second thought to the need for some yardstick to measure the performance of a $60,000-a-year sales manager or plant superintendent.

In my observation of hundreds of companies representing widely diversified industries, I have been continually amazed at the number of executives who are paid high salaries for expertise in executive analysis yet still fail to recognize that management cannot always be permitted to march to the beat of its own drummer. In some instances this policy of regarding managers as a superelite group who are exempt from the same set of standards that they apply to subordinates can be charged to simple ego. More often than not, however, it is caused by a failure to recognize how much an organization has expanded. Subtly and imperceptibly, operations often get too big and complex to be guided by the random advice and counsel of whatever select hierarchy happens to be situated near the top of the administrative totem pole at the moment. When this happens it is time for management to realize that it can no longer afford the luxury of operating under an industrial caste system. At that time accountability standards must be developed, not only at the lower rungs of the administrative echelon but for all members in the organization.

Failure to recognize the need for executive accountability can sometimes be attributed to management advisors who, to put it bluntly, are brought in to find out what went wrong by the people who made it go wrong. Even when these management advisors recognize the problem, they are often reluctant to criticize the people who pay their fees. I'm not claiming that this is standard practice among all management advisors, but it happens often enough to constitute a real problem in many organizations.

The time is long since past when any organization can meet the competition with a random set of rules based on the dubious premise that management can be depended on to do the right thing simply because it had been vested with the authority to make decisions. At some point in an organization's development, whether it be through mergers, growth, diversification, or increased competition, a company can no longer put up with a game plan that entails outguessing the competition. Instead, the competition must be *outplanned*. Management must also be held accountable for both making and executing plans. Put another way, planning, unless accompanied by accountability, is as worthless as the message in a Chinese fortune cookie.

Long- and Short-Range Planning

Two extremely fashionable subjects these days are long- and short-range planning. Enough literature has been written on both of these subjects to fill a good portion of the Grand Canyon. And, sad to state, as far as attaining the intended results is concerned, much of this material might as well have been dispatched directly to that location.

I'm not suggesting that planning is not necessary to the financial stability of an organization. Most financial institutions today require and demand that a company have a long-range planning program before they will grant a loan. All too often, however, planning projects go down to defeat after the first few skirmishes because they are poorly conceived, are inadequately implemented, and fail to include the proper degree of individual responsibility. It is also vitally important that the program be thoroughly sold to those people responsible for its success.

Each company is a unique entity, not only because of the people who make up its personnel, but also because of its environment, the organization itself, its products, the industry in which it operates, and the resultant conditions of change. Therefore, for any planning project to acquire an acceptable degree of success requires an awareness of all these conditions coupled with a thorough understanding of the general criteria of effective implementation.

Development of a viable planning program is not something that can be done as an interesting interlude between sales meetings. It is a difficult and complex endeavor that can be successful only if it is pursued vigorously over an extended period of time. Most short-range planning projects will have a duration of one year, or possibly longer. In the case of long-range planning, the program usually extends for five years. It is the uncertain developments that occur during this lengthy time span that cause many planning projects to gradually deteriorate and eventually disintegrate under their own weight when well-intentioned goals and objectives are sabotaged by unforeseen problems and unexpected developments.

For the company that wants to begin planning but hasn't done it up to now, evolution is too slow and revolution is too fast. Therefore, one significant question arises: Is there any sure-fire method by which an organization can embark on a planning project and be assured of favorable results?

The answer to this seemingly loaded question is an emphatic yes! Such a program does exist and can virtually guarantee results. It is a program that was specifically designed to address and cope with the weaknesses that have been all too common in planning projects in the past. The method that I am about to describe has been used successfully by numerous large and small organizations with results that more often than not exceed original estimates. Like most effective devices it involves some groundwork, coordination, and more than a soupçon of tenacity. But for those who are willing to pay this price it is a program that comes as close to guaranteeing results as any management tool I have ever seen. For lack of a better term I call this method "Assuring Results Through Accountability." The balance of this chapter will consist of a comprehensive outline of exactly how this program works.

The Assured Results Planning Program

In all types of industrial operations over the years, I have noted only one universal factor that separates the outstanding companies from ones that are mediocre—top management in the outstanding companies requires and demands accountability of everyone from the janitor to the company president.

Reduced to its simplest form, Assuring Results Through Accountability consists of a step-by-step method for accomplishing assured results, with each step of the process laced with large portions of accountability. Admittedly, establishing and meeting executive standards of accountability are not always easy tasks to achieve. Spontaneous acceptance of the need for increased performance by key people is often a pill that is difficult to digest. But if the steps outlined in this chapter are diligently followed, a successful program can be developed with extremely favorable results. Furthermore, the people who might initially regard the program unenthusiastically often turn out to be its biggest backers.

Most planning programs fall apart for a variety of reasons in addition to failure to include a proper degree of accountability. In designing a program, many managers fail to take the time to find out exactly where they are at present and where they intend to go. In some instances program goals are assigned to subordinate managers on the basis of personality traits rather than on the basis that management behavior is more important than personality. Additionally, goals and objectives are frequently based on meaningless criteria and fuzzy concepts that do little to describe the actual improvement required or the time frame in which this must be accomplished. Still other pitfalls include failure to lay proper groundwork, to secure motivation, to adequately describe organizational responsibilities, and to delegate the proper degree of authority.

Assuring Results Through Accountability is specifically designed to eliminate all these common problems. It consists of five separate steps: developing a management inventory, developing corporate objectives, establishing goals, converting goals to specific projects, and assuring the program's success.

For purposes of clarification, the term "objectives" as used in this text refers to corporate objectives as set forth by top management and/or the board of directors. "Goals" refer to the agreed-upon targets to be accomplished by individual managers within the organization. "Projects" refer to the ways and means of accomplishing these goals.

These steps can be implemented most effectively if they are performed separately in the order shown. In some instances, however, where no lines of authority overlap, it may be logical and expedient to proceed to the next step in a department or division before all the details of the previous step have been finalized by the entire organization.

Either way, the first step in the program should be developing a management inventory.

Developing a Management Inventory

Whether it is conducted as a massive project in a large corporation like General Motors or as a superficial check by a small shopkeeper, the process of conducting a periodic inventory is an indispensable part of the American business machinery. It is doubtful whether any firm could long survive without this inventory.

Yet while virtually all companies have some form of inventory mechanism, most of them fail to include one component that is vital to the future success of the organization. Specifically, they fail to include a comprehensive listing of exactly where improvement can be most effectively achieved, plus an assessment of what can be expected of individual managers in accomplishing these improvements.

Preparation of a management inventory will do more than simply advise top management of areas where marked improvement can be expected. It will also help convince individual managers that the chief executive officer is serious about the proposed planning project. Additionally, it will generate enthusiasm for the program from managers who in participating in the management inventory will be forced to think about ways the program can be more effectively implemented.

Over the years, numerous planning programs have appeared on the industrial horizon. They go by names like "management by objectives," "management by results," "long- and short-range planning," "standards of accountability," and other titles. Many of these programs are based on generally sound principles and can often be expected to achieve a degree of success. However, in all the books and magazine articles that have been written on this subject, if there is one plan that contains more than a superficial mechanism for determining exactly where improvement can be expected, it has escaped my notice and been conspicuous by its absence.

A planning project can in many ways be compared to a surgical operation. If we accept this analogy we might well ask: "Is there a surgeon today who would attempt to operate without first making a complete examination of the patient's problems?"

In its simplest form, planning consists of determining where we want to go. However, it's extremely difficult to find out where we want to go unless we first know where we are. Hence the need for a management inventory.

A management inventory should consist of a series of questionnaires covering four basic subjects: plant capacity planning, market planning, product planning, and financial planning. Understandably, the actual distribution of these questionnaires, plus the type of questions they contain, will vary somewhat depending on the organization and the types of products or services it offers. Nevertheless, the basic theme should be to permit managers to analyze their present operation coldly and unemotionally, in terms of improvement. In developing the questions, no attempt should be made to obtain simple yes-or-no answers. Rather, the wording should force the managers to think out their replies and give personal views and opinions.

Prior to distributing the questionnaires it should be pointed out to each individual manager that there are no right or wrong answers. They should be assured that the study is designed to stimulate ideas for improvement that can be later converted to goals and then into projects, which, when executed correctly, will help them to reach departmental goals. Additionally, they should be instructed to analyze each situation unemotionally and without regard to personalities except as they directly influence the solution to the problem. They should be informed that the questions have been constructed to stimulate thinking on a wide variety of subjects and the relationships of these subjects to their department. Also, in the event that they feel there are circumstances beyond their control, they should be encouraged to answer frankly.

A list of suggested questions designed for each of the four basic categories noted above follows:

Plant Capacity Planning

1. Please describe the present plan of organization in your department and show the revisions you think are necessary to strengthen or correct weaknesses. Do you believe that all key jobs are adequately staffed and that there is proper strength in the second and third echelons of management? Are there functions essential to present operations that are not yet a part of your organization?

2. Is your industrial engineering department adequately staffed and functioning properly? If not, why not?

3. Explain the strengths and weaknesses of your present work operation area. Do you have a surplus or shortage of floor space? Is there a need to replace major equipment? If so, explain why and estimate its cost. Has the use of other facilities been properly considered? Explain.

4. How recently has your present work area layout been checked? What has been done? What needs to be done? What layout changes would have to be made to *decrease* costs and *increase* production? Explain.

5. Has a program of simplification of paperwork and elimination of forms been instituted? When? Is it effective? How do you know?

6. Has a program to check the effectiveness of tooling been installed? Has it been checked recently? When?

7. Is there an effective program of preventive maintenance? Document results since it has been in operation.

8. If applicable, describe your program for quality control. Is there a scrap control program? What percentage of scrap do you have now as compared to the past three years?

9. Is the inventory control function maintaining stocks of finished goods, raw materials, and supplies at levels adequate to meet production and sales requirements and at the same time avoid unnecessary use of working capital? Describe the method used to insure balanced inventories. What turnover does your department get by major product line

per year? What do you consider good performance? Why? If present performance is not meeting standard, how do you explain it?

10. Is obsolescence of parts checked periodically? What have been the results of this check for the past year?

11. Does our sales department provide our production department with adequate forecasts for production control and scheduling? If not, why not? Describe current programs to improve these forecasts and how they are coordinated with the sales division.

12. Does our plant have the machine-hours and man-hours to permit effective scheduling? If not, what should be done to alleviate this problem? Are parts and operations sheets complete? If not, how should they be modifiied?

13. Is the question of "make or buy" raised periodically? If not, why not? If so, what were the results? Do you feel that purchasing and production are properly coordinated? If not, what should be done to alleviate this problem?

14. Are production standards and/or wage incentives being properly utilized? What percentage of your direct workers are covered? Do you think the present standards or wage incentives are effective for maximum productivity? If not, what should be done to correct them?

15. Is indirect labor covered by standards? If so, what percentage? If not, why not? Is machine downtime recorded and accounted for? How is this done?

16. Are cost figures available by product and by operation? Is the factory cost system functioning as an effective management tool?

17. What has been done to be certain that subordinate managerial and supervisory personnel are aware of company policies?

18. Explain the advantages and disadvantages of your department's program for selecting and upgrading personnel. Are you satisfiied that this is working well? What can you suggest to improve it?

19. Are our plant wage and salary practices in line with our policies and with community rates? Give details if you believe there are problems.

20. Do you have a program for job evaluation? If not, why not? If so, what has been done to be certain it is being maintained? If wage incentives are used, how are they being maintained? Have written policies for their maintenance been established? If so, show examples. If not, why not? Is there a program of merit rating? If so, describe it. If not, why not?

21. Do you know what the present attitudes of your employees are? What methods have you used to determine employee attitudes? Have you taken corrective action on legitimate complaints? What have you done to insure that communications are a two-way street? Does your department have an employee handbook? If not, when will you have one? Is an effective suggestion system in operation? Cite results.

22. What types of training programs are presently in use? What are the strengths and weaknesses of the existing programs?

23. What is your employee turnover and how does it compare with the area and the industry? What can you suggest to improve it?

24. Cite any additional ideas you may have about how our staff can be of more value in helping you attain short- and long-range program goals.

Market Planning

1. Who, or what group in your department, determines the product needs of your department and the markets you serve? Do you feel that this responsibility is correctly assigned at present and that the procedure is working with maximum effectiveness? If so, explain why. If not, explain why not and what you suggest for improvement. Do you feel that there is any corporate or outside influence that is preventing your department from doing an outstanding job in this area?

2. Are you confident that you know the current demand for your major product lines in the markets you serve? What sources do you use to get this information? Do you believe

you and your organization are doing a good job of recognizing new applications for existing products in present or new markets? Why? Do you feel that you can predict total demand and your share of market for major product lines for the next three years with reasonable accuracy? Why or why not?

3. Do you feel that products produced in your department have product superiority over competition? If so, tell why by product line. If not, why not?

4. What do you believe to be the current opinion of your customers about your major product lines? How do you know? Can you define your dollar and percentage share of each major market during the past three years? If so, please do so. If you think customers are critical of one or more of your lines, please describe and give your opinion about why. Can you suggest changes to correct this? What keeps you from making those changes now?

5. Who determines pricing policies for the product lines in your department? How often are prices reviewed? Describe your procedure for setting and adjusting unit and parts prices. If you sell service, how do you determine price? Are you satisfied that you base pricing decisions on adequate information? Explain. What improvements can you suggest for better pricing control and price-setting methods?

6. Describe your policies for functions such as the establishment of credit terms, trade discounts, and quantity discounts. Are these policies clearly defined in writing for your sales group and customers? If not, why not? What evidence do you have that these policies are followed?

7. Who develops sales policies in your division, and how are they communicated to the salesperson level? How do you know that these policies are communicated and understood? What is the method of obtaining sales leads? What are the extent and intensity of supervision of individual sales personnel? Do you think sales techniques and salesperson supervision could be improved? How? What keeps you from doing this?

8. Please list your principal competitors and document

their strengths and weaknesses. What do you believe to be the market acceptance of competitive products? How have you determined this? Describe any abnormal competitive practices. Are you satisfied that your sales management and field groups really know what competitors are offering customers? What evidence do you have that this is so? If you believe improvement is required in this area, what suggestions can you offer?

9. Do you personally participate in forming policy and planning for advertising, publicity, trade shows, and product promotion schemes? How do you rate these programs against similar programs offered by the competition? What could be done to improve them? Do you feel that budgetary or outside influences keep you from doing an outstanding job in these areas? Explain. Is there good coordination between promotion programs and direct selling? Give positive or negative examples.

10. Are you satisfied with the timing and technical quality of bulletins, spec sheets, instruction manuals, service manuals, and parts lists for new products in your department? Explain with examples. If not, suggest improvements.

11. Please state your views in detail concerning the best methods for selection of sales personnel. Are we presently using these methods? If not, why not? Do you believe your sales organization is well balanced from an age and experience level? Give details, please. Can you suggest any improvements you would make if you had a completely free hand?

12. Please state your views in detail on the best methods of training and retaining sales managers and sales personnel. Are you satisfied with our current programs? If not, why not? How do you judge the effectiveness of training methods currently in use? Give examples of existing programs.

13. Describe current methods for forecasting sales by product line and setting individual sales quotas. Do you believe these methods to be effective? How could they be improved? Are you satisfied with your sales call and sales cost-reporting systems? If so, why? If not, why not?

Product Planning

1. Describe the engineering appraisal procedure in use in your department for key engineering personnel. Do you think this procedure is satisfactory? If so, why? If not, what can be done to improve it?

2. What means of communication have been set between engineering, manufacturing, sales, and other departments? Do you feel that current communications procedures are satisfactory? If so, how do you know? If not, why not?

3. What is your basic policy for development of new products and major product redesigns in your department? What major new products have been developed and what have they contributed to annual sales volume in each of the past five years? Please estimate what proportion of the product line volume for the last year came from sale of products not in the line ten years ago. Are you satisfied with this? Why or why not? What steps do you think should be taken to improve your research and product development program?

4. What basic design policies exist in your department and how have you made your organization aware of them? Does the design group give good consideration to manufacturing costs in design? What evidence do you have to support your answer? Does your design group have a good grasp of competitive designs? What's your feeling about this group's peformance compared to your toughest competition?

5. Have you instituted programs between engineering, purchasing, and manufacturing, such as value analysis or substitution of better or less costly materials? If not, why not? If so, what evidence do you have that these programs are paying off?

6. Describe the procedures you have installed for product testing. Have standards been set for product quality relative to practical attainment and competitive products? Give examples. Are you satisfied with existing testing procedures in terms of information obtained and costs involved? What can you suggest for improvement?

7. Can you describe outstanding exclusive features of recent product introductions that you feel indicate above-

average engineering accomplishments? Do you feel that style is being given as large a share of attention as performance? On what do you base this reasoning? How does the competition fare in this area?

Financial Planning

1. Describe how you evaluate international, national, and industry trends and translate your thinking on these matters into departmental actions.

2. Do you foresee major changes in any of the following areas that would have a material effect on your financial planning?

Technology
Customer demands
Competition
Pricing
Taxes
Government regulations

If so, please explain.

3. What steps are being taken to improve the following?
Annual and long-range budgeting
Capital spending estimates
Cash-flow estimates for financial control and cost-system improvement

4. What progress is being made on mechanized machine accounting? Are you satisfied with current efforts? If not, how would you improve them?

5. Are distribution costs under constant review to your satisfaction? If so, what method is used?

6. Are plant expenditures periodically reviewed to determine whether they are justified in view of changing conditions?

7. Are manufacturing expenses controlled through specific budget accounts?

8. Have the insurance requirements of our plant been reviewed for adequacy of coverage, correctness of values, and reasonableness of costs? If not, why not?

9. Are credit and collection policies established and

communicated to marketing? What inadequacies do you feel exist? How do you suggest that they be corrected?

The questions above are not all-inclusive but they give an idea of the basic *types* of questions that should be asked. These questions, you will note, are generally designed to stimulate *thinking* on the part of individual managers on topics that can later be translated into workable goals.

Top management and the people selected to guide the planning program should make a comprehensive review of the composite replies. It will be almost certain to pinpoint areas where improvement can be expected. Armed with a comprehensive list of areas for possible improvement plus a complete inventory of departmental strengths and weaknesses, the person in charge of the planning project will now be in a position to structure the program in a manner designed to insure that agreed-upon goals are consistent with the abilities of the individual managers who will be charged with the responsibility for accomplishing these goals.

Even more importantly, conducting a management inventory as described above will lay the groundwork to enable an organization to develop and implement a planning program based on accountability techniques and tailored to individual managerial thinking.

Developing Corporate Objectives

Before even attempting to establish any future goals for key personnel who participated in the management inventory, it is imperative that top management and/or the board of directors agree on a set of company objectives that can later be used as a basis for developing departmental goals.

The importance of establishing meaningful and workable objectives cannot be overemphasized. Most companies have already established some objectives. However, all too frequently they are based on wishful thinking or superficial data. In some cases, they may even consist of meaningless propaganda designed to pacify the company's stockholders.

To be effective any company objective must be based on

solid, workable data and should conform to the following guidelines:

1. *It must be practical.* Does it really represent a marked benefit for the total organization, or is it simply a sacred cow that has been insisted on by a single section or department?

2. *It must be suitable.* Are you heading in the right direction? You can't set an objective to sell more buggy whips when the nation is going out of the buggy-whip business.

3. *It must be acceptable.* The people who are needed to turn an objective into a reality must be sold on its practicability.

4. *It must be economically feasible.* Is it worth the price in money and man-hours that could be used to better advantage elsewhere?

5. *It must be attainable.* You can't build a spaceship in a blacksmith shop no matter how strong the motivation. The management inventory can be an invaluable tool in determining attainability.

6. *It must be measurable.* Wherever possible an objective should be stated in quantitative terms. "Reduce unit manufacturing cost" is a fuzzy concept. "Reduce unit manufacturing cost from $10.50 per unit to $9.25" is unmistakable and suited to subsequent measurement.

Here is a sample list of corporate objectives that meets all the requirements just described.

1. To utilize the total assets and resources of the company to increase the earnings per share. The objective for the current year is $1.60 per share.

2. To realize a company return on investment of at least 15% of total assets before taxes while generating the maximum cash flow.

3. To grow by investment of capital assets and major expense in new products, by development or acquisition, that increase the corporate return on investment by a minimum of 5%.

4. To spend up to 3% of sales on the development of new and/or improved products to increase our penetration of current markets.

5. To utilize our manufacturing capacities at a minimum average of 50%.

6. To discontinue obsolete and/or unprofitable product lines that represent dying business.

7. To increase market penetration by 5% to 10% depending on product line.

8. To be recognized as Number One in the market for both quality products and services.

9. To recognize the significance of total abilities and total costs when evaluating opportunities for new product development or acquisitions.

10. To recognize the different characteristics of our different kinds of businesses and to find the most effective method of operating each of these businesses within the framework of overall corporate objectives.

11. To diversify by development or by acquisition into added multicustomer markets that meet the prior corporate objectives.

Establishing Goals

Once corporate objectives are firmly fixed, the next step is for subordinate managers to establish goals to meet these objectives. Before this can be accomplished it is absolutely essential to create the proper climate. If the proper climate does not exist, it is doubtful whether the program will ever really amount to much.

Climate encompasses many things. It includes the ability of subordinates to express basic disagreements without reprisals from superiors. It includes a real attempt on the part of supervisors to search for, rather than skim over, possible disagreements between themselves and those under their jurisdiction. It includes acceptance of the fact that managers' stature will not suffer if their thinking is modified by others.

Usually, a chief executive wants to set goals to achieve improvements. Unfortunately, approaching subordinates on that basis will often negate any possible benefits. Top management should refrain from advancing its own ideas, or even suggesting possible goals.

The program cannot be regarded as a necessary evil by the

people who must make it work. The key to success is the magic quality of desire. And instilling this ingredient takes an intensive orientation program in which subordinates can develop an appreciation of what specific goals can do for *them*. The program can be guided by someone else, but management *must* participate, and management *must* be sold on the program.

In this stage the advantages to subordinates, the potential of increased earnings, the spirit of competition, and the opportunity for advancement through company growth can be stressed. The learning process will be more effective if subordinates receive the same reading material that is circulated among top management.

The greatest emphasis should be on the fact that the departmental goals developed to achieve the stated corporate objectives will be set by the person whose performance is going to be evaluated during the course of the program. Once the goals are established, of course, they can usually be rephrased or restated by the chief executive. But if top management sets the standards first, it may abort the entire program.

When working with people who have never set goals before, it is better to give them an overall view of the program in the first session and then give them time to think about it. Several meetings a few weeks apart are preferable to one long session. Because each manager will be responsible for setting his or her own goals, a responsibility checklist must be developed. The list should state exactly which key personnel are to be made responsible for improvement in the various areas where more effective performance is indicated. This list need not be extremely complex, but it should be pertinent to the specific job. If the superior and subordinate prepare the list jointly, it usually turns out to be a developmental experience for both of them. It is important to avoid the pitfall of listing personal traits rather than examining specific issues and end results. No confusion or misunderstanding can be allowed regarding responsibility or authority in any area. Insofar as possible, the organization should strive to avoid overlapping of responsibility or authority by several departments or individuals.

A word of caution here. I recall an old Arabian Nights tale in which the protagonist, a poor peasant boy, was asked about his goals in life. He said he wanted to become the richest man in the kingdom, become ruler of the entire empire, and marry a princess. In the story he attains all three of these goals. This, of course, was only a fairy tale. I cite it to point out that one of the pitfalls in permitting managers to set their own goals is that, contrary to what you might expect, they often set them too high. Their optimism in some instances may be sparked by a genuine enthusiasm for goal-setting. Or in other cases it may result from the simple desire to tell top management something they feel it would like to hear. In either case this can be a built-in booby trap, particularly if top management compounds the problem by accepting a set of next-to-impossible guidelines. Problems will develop later when the initial guidelines must be modified, because this may set a precedent for watering down the entire program.

The real catalyst that makes a program successful is strict accountability. Members of the organization should all be fully aware that they are in business for themselves. It is also important to hold regular meetings, preferably monthly, to insure that the timetable for goal setting is being maintained. Since the goals were set by the individuals responsible for maintaining them, contingencies should have been taken into account. In other words, there is no acceptable excuse for nonperformance!

Once departmental goals are tentatively established, it is important at this point for top management to review the goals developed for each department or division to insure that their sum total adds up to the corporate objectives established earlier.

Converting Goals to Specific Projects

When I functioned as a professional director, it disturbed me to note that the designers of most long- and short-range planning programs end their efforts when the design stage is over and hope that subordinates and key personnel will be sufficiently motivated and qualified to follow through with the necessary implementation. Unfortunately, it is not that easy. This is the precise point where a program of this type will begin to deteriorate unless additional steps are taken.

Successful implementation of the program requires that the goals established earlier now be converted into specific projects—which frequently may include subprojects. Each project plan will describe the end result to be accomplished in quantitative terms, including the time needed for completion. Benchmarks will have to be established in advance. A six-month project, for example, will contain six benchmarks so that the status of the project can be determined at successive monthly meetings.

Because the problems in various organizations are so diversified it is unlikely that any two could be solved by the same form of remedial action. For the sake of illustration, let's assume that one department in a particular company set a goal of lowering production costs by 15% within the next 12 months. Suppose further that the basis for this goal is that the competition is spending much less on operational costs.

The obvious action must be to translate that goal into specific projects to be finalized as outlined earlier in this chapter. Specific projects for accomplishment of the above goal could be any or all of the following:

Better incentive coverage
Measurement of indirect labor costs
Work simplification program
Standardization of parts
Improved tooling
Better materials handling

Even the most superficial analysis of these six projects will determine that most of them will also involve subprojects. For example, the work simplification program will probably entail a detailed analysis of the work operations performed by all key personnel, including the foremen, the assistant foremen, and the setup workers. It would be conducted by the staff engineering department from headquarters and would also include a value analysis program by the plant industrial engineering department. Staffing tables would have to be developed by staff industrial engineering, along with cost estimates, techniques of accomplishment, and a quantitative outline of what had to be accomplished in a fixed period of time.

Because of the complex nature of achieving many of these goals and projects, it is imperative that a logical step-by-step procedure be set up at this time to accomplish the pre-stated aims and assure successful implementation of the program. The following step-by-step procedure has been used successfully by many companies and is recommended for assuring that the program will achieve the desired results.

Assuring the Program's Success

Immediately following the establishment of departmental goals, a meeting should be held with all department heads. At this meeting these key managers should be informed that they will have many problems to solve in meeting their respective goals. For example, if the vice president of operations has a goal of reducing labor cost by 15% in the next 12 months, he or she will have the problems of scrap control, reducing both direct and indirect labor, and reducing overtime costs.

The managers should then be informed of the steps to be taken to accomplish these goals and how to resolve the problems that may arise during implementation of the program. Each company goal or problem encountered as part of that goal must be interpolated into projects in the following manner:

1. Obtain a thorough, detailed description of the problem.
2. Determine and describe what is to be accomplished.
3. Determine if there are any subprojects needed to ac-

complish the primary project. If so, assign a person or people to determine subprojects.

4. Determine the technique of accomplishment. It is very important to think this through, for many reasons. If this is not done it will be difficult to determine the man-hours needed to accomplish the project and also to schedule the completion date.
5. Carefully determine the man-hours needed to complete the project.
6. Establish a cost estimate to complete the project.
7. Estimate savings or nonmonetary results.
8. Place priorities on multiple projects.
9. Establish benchmarks. If the project is to take six months, six specific benchmarks must be determined in advance, in order to determine the status of projects at succeeding monthly meetings.

During this same meeting the managers should be cautioned to be certain to analyze each project thoroughly and completely for possible subprojects and for possible problems that could change the time schedule or overall results. They should also be warned to allow adequate time and to look out for necessary information required from other people or departments. They must be certain that projects represent genuine improvements, not just a part of day-to-day operations, and that not too many projects are undertaken. Managers must make sure that everyone involved understands all the implications of the project, and that all concerned are prepared to meet unforeseen difficulties that may tend to stand in the way of completing the project in the indicated time frame. Finally, managers must see that all employees, including subordinates, have gone through the same thorough analysis process to insure that they, in turn, will accomplish the desired end results.

A second meeting should be held in approximately three to four weeks, at which time each member will make a presentation of his or her project or projects, a definition of what is to be accomplished, an identification of any accompanying subprojects, a comprehensive overview of how the project will be accomplished, a presentation of the monthly benchmarks, and a statement of the final completion date. During this second meeting all members should be reminded that each member has been permitted to determine his or her own method by which to accomplish the end results. Each member has been permitted to determine his or her own time schedule, and each member has been permitted to determine what and how much is to be accomplished. Therefore no excuses will be acceptable for not accomplishing end results since each person has been given adequate opportunity to allow for contingencies. For maximum effect, this speech should be made by the president or a delegate of the president.

During the rest of the program, meetings should be held on a schedule geared to the benchmarks that were determined earlier. At these meetings, members should present the current status of their projects. Throughout the entire program it should be emphasized at each meeting that the individuals involved have complete responsibility for their part in the program and will be evaluated on their ability to carry out their self-established goals.

If top management reiterates this policy at *each* meeting, lower-level managers will be extremely reluctant to risk embarrassment in front of their peers, to say nothing of possibly jeopardizing future status within the organization, by failing to meet goals. However, in the event that one or more of the members should attempt to present excuses for falling behind schedule, it is important that the chief executive or other top management not fall into the trap of reprimanding the person or expressing disappointment at his or her nonperformance. To do so would imply taking the responsibility off the manager's back. Instead, a simple statement like: "Sorry to hear that, Joe. You're aware, of course, that this is *your* project. Now, what are you going to do to alleviate these problems?" will almost always get the project back on the track again.

Once the program has been completed, a performance review should be conducted for all employees involved, together with a thorough analysis of the program's results. This can set the stage for a new program to be developed in the same manner.

Program Benefits

Assured Results Through Accountability as outlined in the preceding pages was initially developed when I was retained as a professional director and advisor to the president and/or the board of directors in several manufacturing organizations. In this capacity I had to initiate a program that would insure that the agreed-upon objectives would be met. To do this it was obvious that I would have to lay out the road map for the program. I would not be in a position to give orders, so I must instead rely on positive direction. I would have to get results through other people, and I would have to assure the end results.

The program *will work*. The potential advantages for organizations that are willing to take the time and trouble to implement a program of this type are so obvious that I sometimes wonder why everyone isn't using it. To name a few:

1. Assured Results Through Accountabilty represents a programmed road map built around real data and facts such as due dates, percentages, and dollar volume. This brings results.
2. Because the program is based on individual accountability, it gives the chief executive the opportunity to utilize time more effectively on more important areas of the business.
3. It provides the opportunity to check real progress continuously, in total, or by division specifically, as required.

In addition to the immediate rewards provided by a positive management approach, there are several long-range benefits that will almost certainly be acquired.

1. The program encourages sound decision making at all levels.
2. It develops and forces a closer understanding of problem solving through better communications between executives and subordinates.
3. It furnishes a clearer understanding of individual action as a part of group action.
4. It provides an unusual vehicle for developing greater individual achievement and gives an incentive for this achievement.
5. It provides the logical, sound basis for an integrated management-by-direction program.
6. It provides guided direction aimed at upgrading executive performance from fair to good and from good to outstanding.
7. It forms stepping-stones to long-range planning.

Yes, There Can Be Problems

It should be obvious at this time that the step-by-step program outlined in this chapter is based primarily on a strong code of managerial accountability. There is no built-in mechanism for failure. Because of this, it is important that the goals and projects agreed upon are achievable. The program cannot function if top management, in its zeal to acquire maximum results within the shortest possible time span, allows itself to be trapped into approving impossible standards based on wishful thinking or blue-sky expectations.

With this in mind, I'd like to close this chapter by being completely candid and sharing with you some of the errors and blunders I have made in installing earlier programs of this type, in the hope that you will not have to experience them yourself.

1. Since Assuring Results Through Accountability is a continuing effort, do not allow your subordinates' goals to be too difficult the first time around. Most managers will set their goals too high. It is very important that your subordi-

nates succeed on the first go-around. It must, however, be a challenge.

2. Do not allow everyday responsibilities and requirements to enter into goal or project development.

3. Do not allow any individual manager to have too many projects.

4. Be certain that each manager thinks through his or her project thoroughly and completely. Be sure not only that all the manager's subordinates are involved, but that they program their own subprojects. A chain is only as strong as its weakest link.

5. If there are too many goals, be certain to eliminate unnecessary ones. It is better to accomplish a few more important ones than to partially accomplish many.

6. Last, but most important: As long as the employee determined the goal, how it was to be accomplished, what the end result would be, and in what period of time it would be completed, be firm in the policy that you have every right to expect the end result that was initially established. *No excuses.* The participants are expected to provide for contingencies!

The program outlined in the preceding pages involves a little more time and effort than the typical planning programs used by most companies. However, on the basis of my observations over the years, I can safely say that 80% of the other long- and short-range plans I have seen never accomplish their intended objective. This is because of the two factors mentioned on the first page of this chapter, namely (1) management fails to take the time and trouble to make a thorough management inventory, and (2) the program lacks a practical method to insure that the goals will be met. With the ever increasing proliferation of management jobs in American industry, accountability is an ingredient that is not only necessary but virtually mandatory if an organization is to survive.

seven

Putting Direction in the Board of Directors

Dreadful things are just as apt to happen when unknowledgeable people control a situation as when ill-natured people are in charge.

Don Marquis

The role of the corporate director has in most instances remained virtually unchanged since the turn of the century. Despite the increasing tempo of operations and growing specialization brought about by quantum jumps in industrial technology, the corporate director is too often only a figurehead, duly listening as corporate policy is enunciated and nodding on appropriate cue. His official duties consume four or five hours of meeting time each month or quarter, for which he is charitably rewarded. Overall performance is graded primarily on attendance records.

The ritual is repeated with monotonous regularity for the purpose of reassuring company management that it enjoys the confidence and support of the panel that ostensibly represents the company owners. The really important factors, however, are normally the prestige and vanity of the directors themselves, many of whom do not represent or serve the owners or, for that matter, anyone but themselves.

128

A major contributing factor to this alarming condition is the fact that many board memberships are awarded for the wrong reasons. Appointment to a board is often contingent upon personal friendships or desire to lend the board an air of respectability, rather than on ability to perform. In some instances this may be a calculated device to load the board with individuals who are reluctant to make waves. More often, however, it is based on a failure to recognize the full extent of a board member's potential impact on the organization.

State laws of incorporation normally confer broad powers upon directors. They may declare dividends; approve policy matters such as mergers and acquisitions; establish policy concerning audits, financing, and general expenditures; change corporate by-laws; select operating managers; establish executive salaries; and perform many other important functions. Yet despite these inherent powers many boards today, by the most charitable definition, are mediocre bodies that resemble arid deserts of untapped talents, unfulfilled capabilities, and misplaced hopes.

In fairness to the people who, in good faith, agree to serve on these boards, it must be stated that in many instances the lethargy evidenced by many board members is not of their own choosing. It is caused primarily by the procedure through which most boards are selected. In too many cases the job of being a director is incidental to the primary vocation of the individual concerned. Often people are placed on the board simply because their names lend prestige to a company.

In a staff report put out by the Judiciary Committee of the House of Representatives, a tabulation was prepared concerning the status of directors serving at 74 leading companies. Within these 74 companies, 146 directors served on 20 or more boards, 228 served on 15 or more, and 307 on 10 or more!

For the people in these positions to fulfill their obligations for any one of the companies they represent, to say nothing of taking care of the needs of their own business or profession, comes as close to an exercise in futility as trying to bail water with a sieve. To further hamper their performance, frequently there is a tacit agreement between top management and the board that board members will function only as figureheads. Often this occurs when strong or dominant presidents feel that they have all the answers and resist outside interference, or when a company is run by a family or selfish interests who are willing to sacrifice efficiency of operation for corporate domination.

In either event, the end result was summed up eloquently by Martin Stone, chief executive officer of Monogram Industries, who stated in an article published by *Business Week* May 22, 1981, "Too many directors are not in a position to learn enough about a company to serve responsibly. At best they acquire a smattering of knowledge and become only a mild irritant and an occasional nuisance."

In recent years some efforts have been made to strengthen the usefulness of the board. Most of these have proven palliative only; others are even contradictory. Some corporations rely exclusively on an "inside board" composed exclusively of the firm's management. In theory, at least, the inside director brings an intimate knowledge of company operations to board meetings. The built-in problem here is whether an organization can expect true independence or objectivity from a board member who is hired, promoted, appraised, and rewarded by existing management. As one inside board member put it: "It's difficult to generate any wild enthusiasm among inside board members over challenging a proposal which has just been advanced by the man who pays your salary." Also, an inside board composed of members representing diverse portions of an organization may frequently be prone to lobbying for items that serve their individual interests, rather than representing the company as a whole.

In an effort to insure a balance of power, some companies have opted for a compromise arrangement where the board is made up of both inside and outside members. Unfortunately, this too often generates some king-sized problems. The major difficulty is that boards of this type tend to be dominated by insiders who are closer to the pulse of the operation and are admittedly more knowledgeable concerning its problems and needs.

An alternate but little-used variation of the mixed board consists of a top tier of outside directors and employee representatives, and a lower tier of inside management employees. The top tier outranks the lower tier and, in effect, supervises the company's supervisors. In theory this insures that inside directors do not dominate the board. Performance records on two-tiered board membership tend to be sketchy. The best statistics on this come from West Germany, where the practice has been prevalent for many years. According to recent reports it has not been an overwhelming success. In fact, many West German corporations are now reverting to more conventional methods.

The basic fault with all these reforms is that they fail to come to grips with the real problem: how to obtain knowledgeable people who will devote a sufficient amount of time to make a significant contribution to the operation.

A contributing factor to the general impotence of the board of directors seems to be the aura of mystery that usually enshrouds board membership. Little known, half understood, often held in awe by those below the policy-making level, "The Board" is often regarded as a corporate Supreme Court that is above reproach and therefore an unlikely target for reform.

In recent years, owing primarily to a number of fiascos allegedly brought about by ineffective board performance, there have been a marked interest and a number of court actions concerning irregularities on the part of board members. Yet a series of court rulings has done little more than evolve some broad guidelines for effective directorship. The most significant of these rulings is the so-called business judgment rule, which states that a board member must exercise the same degree of care that a prudent businessman would show in similar situations. Stated another way, board members are not liable for honest mistakes in judgment but may be accountable if they have been careless.

In an era when American business is beginning to rely more and more on a strict code of accountability, it was perhaps inevitable that some new methods would be devised to upgrade the performance of the board of directors to a level where it is better able to cope with the problems of modern industry. The changes have come about primarily during the past decade, and they were motivated by the realities of increased legal responsibility and perhaps a sincere desire to put to rest the clearly outmoded "buddy system" of a bygone era.

The Committee-Oriented Board

Many of today's larger companies are rapidly reverting to a committee-oriented board composed of members who represent diverse backgrounds, some of whom might even have acquired their expertise outside the world of business. A board of this type requires a keen sense of balance to insure that members of individual committees are better equipped than the board as a whole to deal effectively with issues regarding their particular area of expertise. These committees will vary from one company to another, depending on individual needs. A board may contain an audit committee, an executive committee, a finance committee, a legal affairs committee, a compensation and pension committee, a personnel management committee, and so on.

The most common of these is the audit committee, whose members will probably have a long and varied background in finance or general management. A member of an audit committee is almost always an outsider who often will sit on several other boards in the same capacity. He or she should be independent of management and free from any relationship that could interfere with independent judgment. Ideally, the audit committee should have the power to direct and supervise an investigation into any matter brought to its attention, including the right to retain outside counsel in connection with an investigation. In the light of some recent corporate improprieties, the need for such an entity is obvious—so obvious, in fact, that since June 1978, a policy of the New York Stock Exchange requires that all domestic, publicly owned companies listing securities on the New York Stock Exchange must, as a condition of listing, establish an audit committee composed of members independent from the board of directors.

Another area of specialization by the board of directors in many companies is a public responsibility committee, sometimes alternately referred to as a public issues committee, a corporate responsibility committee, or a people resource committee. The need for a specialized group of this type has been generated, for the most part, by increased emphasis on social issues that affect a company. These could include adverse media publicity, environmental problems, affirmative action lawsuits, consumer boycotts, employee benefits, and other problems that would tend to usurp a large portion of the time and effort by the full board but could be turned over to a committee of four or five members who are particularly skilled in these areas. Members of a public responsibility committee may be either inside or outside members, but they are usually outsiders, some of whom may not be strong in actual business experience but possess a background in things like sociology or public opinion analysis.

On the basis of this type of expertise the public responsibility committee can initiate independent investigations and subsequently make recommendations to the full board based on competent analysis of the issues involved. The public responsibility committee, as a tool for upgrading the effectiveness and efficiency of the board, is now being used by many large corporations, including Sears, Roebuck, General Electric, American Telephone & Telegraph, Dow Chemical, General Mills, and many other blue-chip companies listed in the *Fortune* 500.

The committee concept has caught on exceedingly well in recent years and has been a large factor in obviating what in the past was frequently a hodge-podge of widely diversified opinions from members who had little knowledge of specific issues.

One company that has had considerable success with the committee-oriented board is Connecticut General Insurance Corporation of Hartford. In addition to an audit committee, Connecticut General retains on the board several other committees, all of which comprise individuals who possess expertise in the areas to which they are assigned. Among the committees maintained by the board at Connecticut General are:

1. A financial resources committee, whose purpose is to meet approximately every other month and report to the board on the management of the corporation's financial resources. Its activities include review of the adequacy of capital resources and inquiry into current and planned utilization of capital and the corresponding risk/reward relationships. Additionally, the financial resources committee is responsible for reviewing and reporting on management's recommendations concerning dividend payments to stockholders; changes in the corporation's capital structure; divestment, diversification, or acquisition; bank lines of credit; and other matters involving the commitment of financial resources on which board approval is sought.

2. An investment committee, whose purpose is to meet twice a month to review and report to the board on the management of the investments of the company and its subsidiaries. It is the function of this committee to assure itself and the board that investments are being managed prudently and effectively. This committee reviews and approves investment policies, investment guidelines, and schedules of authority for making investment decisions. It also periodically examines the processes used to insure that these policies, guidelines, and schedules are being followed.

3. A committee on directors, which meets once each year and at such other times as might be necessary to assure itself and the board, through appropriate inquiry and review, that the chairman of the board is effectively managing the development and maintenance of the board's membership and organization. To accomplish this the committee inquires into the work of the chairman of the board in this area to whatever depth is necessary and reports to the board as a whole.

Greater participation by the board in an era when corporate dealings are becoming increasingly complex is clearly long past due. The increasing use of the committee-oriented board has resulted in a marked improvement from the conventional board, which, unfortunately, is still widely used, particularly in smaller companies.

For obvious reasons, the mode of operations of the committee-oriented board may vary widely from one company to another, depending on personalities and the nature of the problems involved. However, as pointed out by Courtney C. Brown in his book *Putting the Corporate Board to Work,** the use of committees "adds a dimension of mature judgment during the process of analysis and appraisal that would otherwise be unavailable. It would assure a comprehensive discussion at the full board meeting of both the positive— and the negative—aspects of a given issue. It would help board members become familiar with management personnel in the junior and middle, as well as the senior, grades. Finally, it would establish a record of participation and supervision that would be hard for critics of the corporation and its procedures to challenge."

Unfortunately, the committee-oriented board functions best in larger corporations that have numerous specialized problems and the financial ability to acquire the multifaceted expertise that is required from widely diversified sources. For the smaller and medium-size companies, however, there is an alternative that is rapidly becoming integrated into the American business system. This involves retaining a working, or professional, director as a member of the board.

The Working Director

Admittedly the working director has not yet developed into a mandatory requirement in America's corporate structure. Nevertheless, the need for some new type of board member in smaller and medium-size companies has reached a point where many corporations are taking a long, hard look at the advantage and disadvantages of acquiring such a professional.

The concept of the working director can be briefly stated. The company elects to its board a director whose responsibility is one of deeper involvement than that of the other members. This person spends a substantial amount of time each month on the job, becoming very familiar with the

*New York: Free Press, 1976.

company, its personnel, its operating methods, and its prospects. As an outsider, such a director brings to the company an indispensable element—objectivity. As an adopted insider, he enjoys the voting rights, privileges, obligations, and burdens of board membership. His duties are to probe, to question, to advise. If he discharges his responsibilities conscientiously and with competence, he can make the board of directors—and the company—vastly more effective and profitable.

Although the operation differs somewhat in principle, the concept of the working director probably originated in Great Britain, where a member of the board frequently also functions as a company manager and where only nominal distinctions exist between directors, managers, and executives.

According to a survey conducted by the Institute of Directors in London, 67% of its members describe their work as being predominantly that of a general manager. Only 10% of those queried regarded themselves as "whole-time directors." This tends to support the theory that British business is run to a large degree by professional managers and executives. An interesting sidelight to this is that British board members also tend to confine their directorships to fewer companies. Only 20% of them hold two or more directorships and only relatively few are members of several boards.

Working directors in America, while functioning somewhat differently from their overseas cousins, first appeared informally on the industrial scene some years back and probably evolved from the favorable results that were achieved when a particular board member decided to assume duties and responsibilities far in excess of what was actually expected.

A More Professional Member

In contrast to both their inside and outside contemporaries, working directors in America are retained as professionals—paid to do the director's job, and even something more. With the blessing of the chief executive officer, the working director peeks and probes and performs in areas where an outside board member would not normally be welcome. On the other hand, directors do not execute policy. Instead they work and get results *through other people.* Ideally this keeps them from becoming bogged down in administrative details, and it obviates accusations of meddling in operating routines.

The advantages of retaining a working director, as opposed to a conventional director, can best be summed up by listing the duties, responsibilities, and limitations that go with the job.

1. *The working director brings a fresh viewpoint to the board.* The viewpoint of the working director differs from that of the conventional director by an entire dimension. Typical outside directors may admittedly possess open minds and an uncompromised attitude. Nevertheless, they can act only on facts that are presented to them by insiders. Their decisions are therefore only as good as the information that they are spoon-fed. Working directors do not rely solely on "official" sources for their information. They initiate inquiries and conduct forays of their own. Outside directors, even if they took the trouble to explore on their own, would scarcely be in a position to follow through effectively.

2. *The working director pinpoints problems before they erupt.* The working director is a familiar figure who pops in and out at will and who speaks to (but does not give orders to) corporate personnel at all levels. Because of this he has an opportunity to prescribe preventive medicine that may obviate ultimate surgery. Additionally, he can be of particular help in the fields of his own special competence, such as finance, labor relations, work measurement, or personnel.

3. *The working director concentrates on policy making and whether personnel apply policies wisely to existing operations.* Because of this he is in an extremely favorable position to advise both the chief executive and the board on policy matters and personnel problems.

4. *The working director contributes experience, knowledge, know-how, and contacts from many diverse sources.* Unlike the

conventional director, he has a background that is rich in many different disciplines. He is familiar with the mores of many management professions and acquainted with the problems and prospects of entire industries. Except for the most gifted people, inside directors are severely handicapped when unfamiliar problems are encountered, such as diversification or acquisitions. A working director is equipped to rise above these limitations. The factors necessary to sound business practice, fortunately, are so nearly uniform that a working director can function effectively in several unrelated industries. In fact there are often advantages to analyzing one business in the light of others.

5. *The working director stimulates the president and other top-echelon executives to better performance.* By virtue of his office, the working director works closely with the chief executive and other top-level executives, serving as a confidential advisor, idea source, and sounding board. He may also, on occasion, act as the devil's advocate to the top company officers.

6. *The working director's position assures that his voice will be heard.* Middle managers reporting to the board are normally bound by propriety and self-interest to lobby for their points of view with the utmost subtlety. Outside consultants must sell their ideas to the board. The working director, however, speaks as a peer among peers. He cannot be misquoted. His views are treated with respect. What's more impressive, he has a vote to back them up. In short, his continuity of relationship permits him to assume responsibility for results.

Organizational Relationships

To be truly effective the working director should always be selected by the board's dominant or controlling group. Consequently, he represents the company's governing faction, and in a sense helps keep it in control. At first glance this may not seem entirely desirable or even advisable. "Where then," we might ask, "is his independence?"

In practice, however, the working director puts his objectivity at the disposal of those in charge. To do otherwise would place him in a functional vacuum—or even worse, pit him against the majority. Actually, the fact that the working director is selected by the controlling group should cause no raised eyebrows. After all, this is the identical route by which the conventional director arrives on the scene. All that differs is the mode of operation.

The working director must work closely, even intimately, with the company's chief executive officer. It is the president's word, after all, that opens doors to the working director and gives him carte blanche to peek, probe, and perform. This type of close relationship will vastly multiply his effectiveness. Because of this special and perhaps unique relationship, some proprieties must be observed. The president, for example, must provide the working director with the same operating and financial data that the principal executives receive.

The director should never initiate an investigation without informing the president of all findings. Suggestions and recommendations acquired as a result of these investigations must be brought to the attention of the president and no other executive. To be completely effective a working director should always take a stand on an issue. He should never avoid a decision even when this decision conflicts with that of the chief executive officer.

For all his right to dig through the corporate structure, talk to lower-echelon personnel, and examine existing procedures, it should be emphasized that the working director functions on the policy level only. Because of this unique status, selection of an individual who can successfully fit into this critical role can sometimes be difficult. If the wrong person is selected, the problems that are generated can often outweigh the benefits derived.

Criteria for Selection

A basic qualification for the successful working director is that the person selected be more concerned with managerial behavior than personality. Since he must get results through other people, he cannot afford to indulge himself in personal grudges or become actively involved in departmental feuds. Instead, his role should be more like a catalyst between operating management and the board of directors. In this capacity he can act as a motivating force, helping officers and key personnel to establish their own goals.

In companies where a working director has acted as a viable addition to the staff, the three most important ingredients for this position are:

1. The ability to arouse the enthusiasm of officers and key personnel.
2. The ability to stay in the background and allow executives to receive full credit for their results.
3. The ability to differentiate between the important and the unimportant. The man who swats at flies while standing in a pit full of crocodiles is clearly out of his depth in a position of this type.

A special type of climate is required to make a working directorship succeed. First, the director must possess unique qualities of personality, character, and experience. He must have an analytical mind, a sound business background, an ability to work with and through people, a willingness to needle top executives into self-examination, a flexible attitude that adapts to different corporations and industries, and finally, a willingness to forgo praise and credit in deference to the operating managers.

The company must possess certain characteristics, too. Among them, its president must be willing to accept criticism, agree to identify problems, and admit that corporate performance can always be improved. He must be willing to act on recommendations advanced by the working director.

Establishing this unique brand of rapport is not always easy. The director may even find that it is not always advisable to accept offers of directorships. In one instance, for example, a working director rejected a seat on the board of a company with sales of $20,000,000. The business was highly successful, sales were at unprecedented levels, profits were strong, and the outlook unclouded. There was just one problem. The president's self-confidence was pitched so high that others could no longer get through. Under these circumstances the working director would have been as functionless as snowshoes in August. In another case a directorship was rejected because management would not accept the principle of unfettered inquiry. Under such conditions a working director can offer little more than any other member of the board—namely a judgment based on penetrating questions posed at board meetings. On the other hand, with the necessary support, a working director can accomplish much more than lies within the scope of the conventional board member. A single example will suggest the possibilities.

A corporation that had entered the fiscal year $750,000 in the red appointed a working director out of desperation. The person selected for the job went to work on a full-time basis, conducting a detailed and comprehensive study of all facets of the business. His analysis of company facts and figures disclosed that loose wage rates had been permitted to develop over a period of years, but the changes had been so gradual and so subtle that neither management nor the board of directors had been aware of the size of the problem—or if they were aware they ignored it. The working director then assumed the task of explaining the situation to union officials and was eventually able to sell them a new and more realistic wage plan. Once this was adopted the company moved back into the black ink and stayed there.

Since the working director is a relatively new type of professional, there is no clearinghouse for candidates. However, a potential pool of competent working directors is being created out of the increasing number of executives who are retiring from their companies at age 65 or earlier. Because of the difference in individual performance one would hesitate to make a flat statement on the amount of experience required for this position. Nevertheless, it is hard to conceive that anyone would be completely qualified with less than 25 years of experience in business management.

Concerning compensation, ordinarily the working director should be paid a retainer instead of an amount per meeting or per diem. There are several reasons for this arrangement. First, the working director cannot predict his working schedule. The amount of time he devotes to a company, like the time a physician gives to a patient, is determined by the characteristics of the case. Also, there is a psychological factor. Under a retainer system, the working director is greeted with pleasure when he arrives at the company and begins to work. Under any other arrangement he is not welcome because each arrival signals that the meter is running and a fee will be charged.

Finally, by working on a retainer basis, a working director achieves the financial independence that nurtures an objective point of view and does not compromise his professional status.

Problems and Pitfalls

While the addition of a working director to any corporate board will, under normal conditions, vastly enhance the effectiveness of that body, there are some problems that can develop, particularly if the wrong person is chosen or if conditions exist that will inhibit his performance.

To expect the director to perform miracles overnight, or under next-to-impossible conditions, is completely unrealistic. As with most managerial tasks, the results attained will be contingent to a large degree on support received from top management and the degree of authority under which he is permitted to operate.

Some basic guidelines that should influence a company's decision about whether or not to retain a working director.

1. *Working directors function best in medium-size companies.* The reason for this is obvious. Larger corporations generally employ teams of internal consultants who, at considerably higher cost, can perform many of the working director's duties. However, such consultants have neither the strong voice in policy nor the close association with the president

that is enjoyed by the professional director. Another limitation posed by a large corporation is geography. A company that has widely scattered branches does not lend itself to conscientious grassroots study.

2. *The working director succeeds only where he is wanted.* When a company is negative toward the idea of having a working director, there is little hope for his success. For example, in one company the president was clearly an egomaniac. His overbearing personality stifled the initiative of subordinates and directors alike. Worse yet, he could not tolerate criticism of the mildest kind. A working director in this organization would have been worse than useless.

Grudging acquiescence and half-hearted cooperation can also be fatal. Genuine enthusiasm, of course, is the ideal requisite. Realistically speaking, however, this emotion is quite rare. Second-best is an attitude of enlighted neutrality and a willingness to give the system an honest test.

3. *The working director's task requires great delicacy to execute in an effective manner.* Unquestionably, the director must be tactful and sincere. He must assure by word, deed, and manner that he is not an inquisitor bent on unearthing scandal or incompetency. Gaining the cooperation of lower-echelon executives is a tedious task. It takes considerable diplomacy to convince all levels that the working director seeks neither glory or gain but works only to upgrade efficiency and boost profits. Laying this groundwork can be time-consuming and requires patience and persistence.

Checklist for the Working Director

Unfortunately, the role of the working director has not yet been fully accepted by American industry. Part of this is probably due to a perverse reluctance on the part of many businessmen to accept change. From a purely objective standpoint some of the reluctance may be justified. After all, in too many instances there are no clear-cut criteria for what a conventional director is supposed to do, and any attempt to further complicate the role of this corporate entity may often be regarded as even further entangling what is already an industrial can of worms.

Nevertheless, a simple look at the areas of usefulness of the average conventional board member as opposed to the potential function of a working director leaves little doubt concerning the need for a person of this type in most organizations. If further proof is needed to support this statement, consider the following checklist prepared specifically for use by a working director and then ask yourself how many of these areas could be effectively probed by a typical member of a conventional board.

A. *Does management operate on a planned and controlled basis, and does it formulate its plans and policies on the basis of adequate factual material and careful study?*

1. Are plans predicated on factual information?
2. Is there any long-range plan to improve the firm's position in the market?
3. Has anybody ever set down on paper a five-year forecast of financial resources and requirements?
4. Is there a long-range plan of product development?
5. Is there a plan for replacement of physical facilities or personnel?
6. Are existing plans predicated on factual information?

B. *Have the company's sales policies and efforts improved and will they continue to improve?*

1. Is the company improving or at least maintaining its position in the industry?
2. Is the industry growing, declining, or static?
3. Is management aware of long-term economic trends within the industry?
4. Is the product line properly designed?
5. Does the product line fit today's market?
6. What is the relationship of the replacement market to the whole?

7. To what extent has the market been abnormally expanded in the past ten years?
8. What is the effect of competitive conditions on normal sales?
9. Is the line designed in such a manner that there are a maximum number of interchangeable parts?
10. Has the line gained or lost customers? Why?
11. Is the line sufficiently diversified?
12. Is the line designed for low production cost?
13. Are sales territories too large or too small?
14. Have sales territories been changed to meet population and buying-power shifts?
15. Do salespeople have adequate incentive?
16. Are salespeople trained to meet the demands of the future?
17. Are the company's prices competitive?
18. Has the company spent enough for promotion?
19. Are present promotion policies effective?
20. Has the sales management inventoried its customers, actual and potential?

C. *Do company facilities and operating methods allow it to compete effectively and profitably?*

1. Are production and inventory control operating properly?
2. Are inventories excessive? If so, why?
3. Are inventories adequate to give good service to customers?
4. Does management know what its breakeven point is?
5. Does management know what to do if sales should drop off sharply?
6. Does management know what to do and what the results would be if a sizable number of orders were suddenly canceled?
7. Does management attempt to budget each executive and supervisor in such a manner that he or she can operate within predetermined limits?

8. Is cost accounting up to date?
9. Is cost accounting meaningful?
10. Is cost accounting used as a tool of control?
11. Is the financial or control department equal to other departments, or is it regarded as "those damn book-keepers"?
12. Can the company compete effectively in production?
13. Is equipment modern and efficient?
14. Is equipment in balance?
15. Is equipment utilized to maximum capacity?
16. Do production delays and inefficiencies result in excessive downtime or setup time?
17. Have standards been maintained?
18. Is the wage incentive effective or has it deteriorated?
19. Have guaranteed wage rates crept in to destroy incentive and control, resulting in excessive labor costs?

D. *Does management operate on a planned and controlled basis and does it formulate its plans and policies on the basis of factual material and careful study?*

1. Does each executive know his or her place on the team?
2. Are major functions such as production, sales, personnel, finance, and engineering properly balanced?
3. Does top management make all the decisions, or is it creating a climate for decision making among the lower echelon in the belief that this is the proper way for managers to develop?
4. Is each major function managed by a competent person, qualified by education, experience, and temperament?
5. If each functional manager does not have one or more potential successors, what needs to be done to develop this succession?
6. Are lines of authority and responsibility clearly defined?

7. Is the organization a harmonious group, or are there those whose self-interests transcend the interest of the management team?

Even a superficial review of the possible areas for improvement that are contained in this checklist will dramatically point up how a working director, endowed with the proper qualifications and authority, can function in situations where a conventional board member would be completely lost. Whether any single individual could function at 100% efficiency in all these areas is, of course, highly doubtful. Being human beings, working directors have their limitations. But if they are honest they will admit their shortcomings when they are unable to define problems or offer solutions, and recommend the necessary procedures to fill the gaps.

In the meantime corporate management, particularly in smaller and medium-size companies, needs to wake up to the fact that the wheels of change are grinding and the clock is ticking. A good, effective board of directors is one of management's strongest assets. It is too important to be allowed to die of obsolescence.

eight

The Business Education Mill—Is It Doing Its Job?

We're poor little lambs
Who have lost our way,
Baa, Baa, Baa.

Excerpt from "The Whiffenpoof Song"

If we accept the altogether logical premise that a sizable number of our productivity problems are generated by ineffective management, fairness requires that we also recognize that many of today's business leaders are desperately concerned with a national trend that appears to be based on a philosophy of getting as much money for as little work as possible.

Why then, we might ask, do not these concerned managers rise up and take more vigorous action to remedy this appalling situation? Is it possible that a large segment of today's management community is simply not equipped either vocationally or temperamentally to cope with the task of successfully managing people?

I realize this is a loaded question to pose in a book aimed primarily at men and women in management. Most managers understandably bristle if told they are unqualified for their present jobs. Nevertheless, I ask that you consider the question objectively and in light of the present academic standards by which many of today's managers are trained.

For the past several decades, careers in management have been one of the most fashionable items in the educational smorgasbord, with the ultimate passport to a good management job being an MBA degree. Each spring, like the arrival of the first daffodil, scores of recruiting executives who represent well-heeled, blue-chip corporations descend on the American universities to participate in the well-publicized Annual MBA Hunt. During this ritual thousands of graduates clutching their coveted MBA degrees in hot little hands are signed up, hopefully for the purpose of infusing new blood into industry's managerial structure.

According to the Association of MBA Executives, graduates with an MBA degree who are employed during this process enter the workforce at an annual median salary of between $20,000 and $22,000.* Some of them have been hired at salaries up to $40,000, reported the December 22, 1975, issue of *Business Week*. (Conversely, students who hold a simple bachelor's degree with a business major average about $13,000.) This, by anybody's yardstick, is an immense salary advantage for a graduate who, in many instances, has never even seen an assembly line in operation. It has not gone unnoticed by the hopefuls who aspire to be our future leaders of business and industry, or for that matter by our institutions of higher learning.

Let's look at some statistics. During the 1960s about 50 well-established schools in the United States were graduating about 5,000 MBA's each year. In 1980 more than 500 schools graduated over 50,000 students.* Exactly what has this tenfold expansion in both schools and graduates done to the chances of a newly minted MBA getting a good position? In

Boston Sunday Globe, November 25, 1979.
*Ibid.

the larger, well-established schools, the answer is "surprisingly little." Competition by businesses for MBA graduates from Harvard, Stanford, and other prestigious colleges is as strong as ever. At MIT there are currently 15 job offers for each graduate, according to the school's dean, William F. Pounds.* Much of this demand is because the prestigious schools have kept enrollment figures fairly constant, and their batting average is maintained by the simple law of supply and demand.

But how about the other schools, many of which were hastily formed and often contain a curriculum based on minimum standards? Exactly what can recruiting executives who hires graduates from one of these institutions hope to get for their corporations' money? The answer to this, of course, depends on the school, and the student. It would be grossly unfair to single out any institution, or group of institutions, as horrible examples. Nevertheless, simply stated, many of the schools today are, by the most charitable yardstick, turning out graduates who are incapable of performing well as managers in a changing environment, under pressures for increased effectiveness, in a world of diminishing resources and higher costs. They continue to be a significant force on the job market primarily because in many cases recruiting executives assume that, if nothing else, the academic standards required to earn an MBA have filtered out some of the flatly unsuitable candidates.

The Need for New Educational Concepts

Back in 1971, J. Sterling Livingston published a now-classic article in the *Harvard Business Review* titled "The Myth of the Well-Educated Manager," which said: "There seems to be little room for doubt that business schools and business organizations which rely upon scholastic standing, intelligence scores, and grades as measure of managerial potential are using unreliable yardsticks."

*Ibid.

The present curricula at most business schools consist largely of academic studies like business economics, managerial accounting, statistical analysis, and other conventional subjects. What is badly needed, however, and is conspicuous by its absence, is a portion of the curriculum that deals with hard business skills like leadership abilities, decision making, business ethics, and other managerial skills that compose a large portion of the everyday work world.

The time is long past due for a new concept in management education that is based on outcome of the education rather than input. So what are we waiting for?

The problem appears to center around the fact that personal managerial skills and abilities are, at best, a fuzzy concept that is difficult to pinpoint and even more difficult to develop at the formal-education level.

The situation is further complicated by a marked difference of opinion between educators and business people concerning the type of interpersonal skills that are needed. This is perhaps predictable. By and large both the educational community and the managerial world tend to be somewhat snobbish about their viewpoints on this subject. People in educational institutions are accused of having an "ivory tower" attitude, and business people are criticized for overemphasizing what they refer to as the real world viewpoint and insisting that this is the only thing of importance.

Despite the bickering, the shortcomings of MBA graduates were brought vividly to light in 1977 by a survey conducted then by the National Center for Productivity and Quality of Working Life. In this survey manufacturing managers of 12 plants ranging in size from 350 to 4,000 employees were asked to rank their college graduates' worth to them in terms of the curriculum they have completed. Rankings of "very useful," "average," and "least useful" were requested. Ten different educational programs were ranked. The results of these rankings are shown in Figure 6.

The surprisingly low ranking (next to last) given to MBA graduates prompted the survey team to inquire about the reasons for the low priority of a subject that is in such high demand. Incredibly enough, the survey respondents' con-

Figure 6. Value comparison of graduates from various curricula.

Type of Degree	Very Useful	Average	Least Useful
Any engineering degree	X		
Mechanical engineering	X		
Industrial engineering	X		
4-year engineering technology	X		
Science with math, chemistry, and physics		X	
2-year technical institution		X	
Business management (BS degree)		X	
Apprentice school		X	
MBA		X	
Liberal arts			X

sensus was that they "had no jobs appropriate to the kind of preparation received by MBA graduates."*

A more blunt appraisal was offered by a disgruntled executive recruiter who stated: "The present curriculum of our institutions of higher learning seems to be based on the premise that the student will become chairman of the board about six weeks after graduation."

Criticism of newly minted business school graduates involves a number of additional factors, all of which tend to inhibit the very productivity improvement these people are supposed to generate. Complaints most frequently noted, according to the same 1977 survey mentioned earlier, include:

*C.A. Anderson, "Summary of Surveys: Education and Industry." Report on a productivity study, presented to the National Center for Productivity and Quality of Working Life, Arlington, Texas, November 18, 1977.

1. They don't associate theory with practice and can't apply knowledge acquired at the academic level.
2. They can't deal effectively with people.
3. They can't write good reports or communicate with subordinates or co-workers.
4. They are impatient and unrealistic. They expect too much.
5. They can't sell their ideas.

Admittedly, the skills that appear to be lacking are ones that do not readily lend themselves to an academic approach. However, there is considerable evidence that business schools are getting further and further away from pragmatic methods in teaching and becoming top-heavy in theory that has little real application to a newly hired administrative assistant who is facing the real management world for the first time.

The separation of business theory and business practice has been intensified even further in recent years by many schools and colleges that, in an effort to meet the demand for new faculty members, have been recruiting teachers primarily from the academic community rather than people with actual business experience.

The AACSB Plan

One of the strongest advocates of the theory that MBA graduates are failing to come up to the needs and standards of modern industry is the American Assembly of Collegiate Schools of Business (AACSB), which is also the national business-school accrediting agency for baccalaureate and master's degree programs in business administration. The agency is presently engaged in a sweeping study designed to determine what student output should be before an MBA degree is granted.

Among other things, the AACSB proposes that all graduating business students take a comprehensive national examination geared not only to academic knowledge but also to personal qualities and characteristics required by an effective manager. To insure that the schools adequately prepare their students for the needs of today's business world, the AACSB further proposes that accreditation of existing business schools be contingent on how their graduates perform in the proposed national test.* If this proposal can be implemented it will eliminate the present accreditation standards under which a school can be accredited simply by offering a prescribed number of subjects taught by an established number of full-time professors who hold an established number of degrees. Instead the accreditation standards of a school will be determined by the knowledge and ability of its students upon graduation.

Adoption of the AACSB proposal would almost certainly thin out some of the MBA mills that have been grinding out graduates with substandard or borderline management skills. It could also give some of the smaller schools without a highly degreed faculty the opportunity for accreditation. Even more importantly, it would raise the level of competence for MBA graduates and perhaps put an end to the current problem of too many MBA's competing for too few jobs. Not surprisingly, the plan has *not* won unanimous approval in the academic community. There is considerable controversy over exactly what type of personal skills should be stressed in the proposed examinations.

In an attempt to cope with this, AACSB advisory panels made up of both business people and college deans have developed a list of 123 attributes for a strong manager. Of these the committee has selected a group of the most significant personal attributes that will almost certainly be weighted in the proposed tests. Some of these, which are almost unheard of in present-day curricula, include decision-making ability; performance stability, including tolerance of uncertainty; work motivation, including energy level; interpersonal skills, including leadership; business values, including ethics; and general mental ability.

*"A Plan to Rate B-Schools by Testing Students." *Business Week,* November 19, 1979.

According to committee members at AACSB, the proposed program will probably not be activated for several years, but it is a definite possibility. In the meantime everything points to the fact that today's accreditation techniques are not adequate. Productivity is being sacrificed because many of today's managers are simply not qualified for the positions they are being paid to fill.

What the Business Schools Say

Predictably, many of the business schools do not share the belief that they are turning out graduates who fail to fit into the demanding role required by today's successful manager. Some comments from the educational community concerning the charges leveled by business people appeared in a November 1980 issue of *Business Week*. In the article Richard N. Rosett, dean of the University of Chicago Graduate School of Business, is quoted as saying: "We do not try to teach them creativity or risk-taking. If their attitudes have not been formed by now, there's not much we can do."

An opinion came from Robert K. Jaedicke, associate dean for academic affairs at Stanford University Graduate School of Business: "It may be that MBA's come out of business schools as potential long-term thinkers but encounter a set of forces that pushes them into short-term thinking."

Another viewpoint on the problem is noted by Alfred E. Osborn, assistant dean of UCLA's business school, who throws the ball back to management by stating: "Businesses are looking for people who are not always critical or disruptive about the way things are. Someone who is arrogant, elitist and tells management that they've been doing everything incorrectly for the past few years is unlikely to be hired."*

In the meantime we appear to be confronted with a situation where business people are becoming more and

*"What Are They Teaching in the B-Schools?" *Business Week*, November 10, 1980.

more disenchanted with the quality of the graduates they hire. And students from our smaller schools who failed to make the grade, yet possess many of the qualities required for successful management careers, can be found driving a taxicab or working in the local post office.

The Elusive Quality of Leadership

What appears to be needed to close the gap between what businessmen need and what they are getting is an educational program designed to stimulate the qualities of leadership.

When I mentioned this to a colleague of mine recently, he readily agreed with me but then hedged his approval with the statement: "It would probably work if only we could get everyone to agree on what is meant by the word leadership." The man, of course, had a point. Leadership means different things to different people. President Ronald Reagan and the Ayatollah Khomeini both possess qualities of leadership, but their approaches toward the problems they face are a world apart—and not just in a geographical sense.

Some years ago in an attempt to define this elusive quality of leadership, I developed and circulated a simple credo that I felt summed up the more important ingredients of the term. Upon reading it over I feel the message is as accurate today as it was on the day it was written. I offer it here as an appropriate way of summing up the qualities needed by an effective manager, with the thought that these qualities are important enough to be included in the education process of any student who aspires to a management position.

A Leader Must . . .

1. Know the important from the unimportant.
2. Be genuinely sincere and reflect it by actions, words, and deeds.
3. Have the right attitude. Success or failure,

happiness or unhappiness are based on the right attitude toward life.

4. Go out of the way to see that subordinates get credit for their suggestions and contributions.
5. Perform today. Procrastination is the cancer of today's supervisors and executives.
6. Admit weaknesses. We all respect someone who makes a genuine effort to do this.
7. Assume an attitude of delivering regardless of circumstances.
8. Try to outguess his or her superior. It's good practice to attempt to perform before a superior makes the request.
9. Carefully consider all the facts before making a decision or drawing a conclusion.
10. Be humble and show it through a good sense of humor. Arrogant people cannot laugh at themselves.
11. Expect performance from subordinates, but always be fair.
12. Face unpleasant tasks head-on. Disadvantage can be turned into advantage by having the courage to face unpleasant facts.
13. Realize that both personal success and the company's success lie in obtaining results through other people. The higher up the ladder a person goes, the more important this factor becomes.
14. Realize the importance of communication.
15. Be willing to stand up and be counted when the chips are down and not sacrifice principles for security.

nine

Bridging the Empathy Gap with Employees and Labor Unions

The art of dealing with people is the foremost secret of successful men. A man's success in handling people is the very yardstick by which the outcome of his whole life's work is measured.

Paul Parker

Historically, the relationship between labor and management has been largely adversary and marked with general suspicion and short-sighted animosity. Thankfully, the goon-squad tactics of a previous era have yielded somewhat to practices like collective bargaining, arbitration, and grievance procedures. Yet an honest appraisal points up the fact that labor and management, in most companies, still regard each other with a smoldering hostility that stems from a colossal lack of understanding and a marked shortage of cooperation by both parties.

Labor's fear of being victimized by unfair management practices is a constant and continual sentiment. Management's suspicion of all labor demands is often a built-in negative factor that divides the two groups into opposing enemy camps. In union shops the hostility surfaces in confrontations at grievance hearings or at the bargaining table. In nonunion shops management frequently lives in fear—sometimes approaching paranoia—that workers might become organized.

In view of the tremendous gains made by labor unions in the past half century, the fear of organization might be a logical management reaction. Nevertheless, if we accept this it seems only fair also to accept the premise that if management would do for unorganized labor what it's forced to do for organized labor, there'd be no need for labor to organize in the first place. It is high time that management took the initiative and stopped reacting negatively to what others set in motion. In many companies today, what passes for an employee relations policy is nothing more than a defensive reaction to forces initiated by others. It took several decades for management to realize that its power was not a God-given right, but a privilege it maintained simply because labor was too weak to reach out and take some of the things that should logically have been its prerogatives.

When labor first began to flex its muscles, many of its demands appeared futile, if not downright amusing. Nevertheless, labor demanded a ten-hour day and got it despite screams of rage that went up from management. There were more screams when labor demanded, and got, an eight-hour day. Now, with management's screams somewhat muffled, some industries already have a 30- to 35-hour week plus other benefits too numerous to mention. During the past several decades labor has done more than improve its lot. It has become the dominant force in American industry.

In addition to the pressures exerted by organized labor, industry must now comply with many laws on the federal and state books controlling practices like hiring, firing, work rules, wage rates, discipline, hours of work, pensions, insurance, and seniority. To their credit, the managers of many organizations have attempted to live with these laws and even make progress in orchestrating a better relationship with employees and labor unions. Unfortunately, it is difficult to orchestrate when an entity like big government is holding the baton.

Laws, of course, can be changed, or made inactive by other laws or amendments. But this takes time—and doing. It's a matter of record that it is easier to get a law on the books than to take it off. It is also infinitely easier to get a clause into a union contract than to get it out. Labor found, in many cases, that trying to change existing laws is time-consuming and mighty expensive. Management, because it is usually regarded as the "heavy" in this scenario, has found it even more difficult.

If we're ready to accept the assumption that the legal status quo changes very slowly, if at all, the logical question that follows is: What can management do within the framework of existing laws to maintain some semblance of its rights and at the same time insure a degree of empathy with the workers who produce its products and services?

To answer this question it is first necessary to pose several additional questions. For example: Can management really blame present conditions on the "big, bad unions"? Or on that crowd back in Washington? Has industry really been taken for a sleigh ride by outside forces? Or is it just possible that management itself willingly relinquished the reins of leadership because it was too apathetic or naive to cope with the opposing forces under their own ground rules?

What, for example, was management doing while organized labor was taking over the store? Did the majority of our industrial leaders ever make a serious effort to assess the real needs of the American worker? Has management, for the most part, ever attempted to create a climate where employees could take problems to their supervisors, instead of a shop steward or union officer? Just what *was* management doing while organized labor was moving into the driver's seat?

The answer to this, sad to state, is surprisingly little, except to maintain a conspiracy of silence at this "upstart group," hoping it would die off and go away.

It should now be obvious to everyone that organized labor isn't going to go away. Nor is it going to easily relinquish the gains it has made during the past 40 years. Why should it? Labor's tactics have been extremely effective—so effective that we might well ask why management hasn't thought of coping with the situation by applying the same general principles. Think about this for a moment: Is there anything that organized labor is doing that management couldn't do just as well?

What Does the Union Offer?

Reduced to a simple sentence, this is the situation: Organized labor has found a king-sized niche in the American business system because it provides what management has failed to provide.

Shop stewards, for example, retain their present role because they have supplemented what the foremen or supervisors should be providing. Stewards are in business because they are able to convince employees that they have the employees' interests at heart. If management, including supervision, possessed this single trait, worker effectiveness and productivity would be sharply increased.

Let's take an analytical look at exactly what the union offers to its members and those who might wish to become members.

1. It pledges wage increases, more benefits, and better working conditions. And it usually comes through with enough improvements to keep the membership quiet.

2. The union keeps its members posted. The information may be union-slanted, and perhaps even a bit inaccurate, but at least the union talks. It *says something*. Management usually says nothing at all, or says very little.

3. The union goes to bat for a member. It gets action on a grievance. When union members have gripes, they usually go to the stewards rather than to their supervisors. Why? Because they can generally get some action out of the stewards.

4. Union membership gives people a chance to participate. They can take part in union affairs and can run for

office. They're not just numbers on time cards. He's Brother Jones; she's Sister Smith.

5. The union offers social activity: beer and bingo for workers and their spouses, and fun for their kids. The hall is a gathering place where workers feel at home.

6. The union treats its members as people. They are visited in the hospital, are helped with roof repairs, and are on the receiving end of a number of acts of personal aid and attention. This makes them feel good.

Read these benefits offered by the union again. Then ask yourself: Would it not be possible for management to perform most of these functions as well as or better than the officials who represent the union? There is little need to state here that few managers have attempted to do this. Assuming that managers truly have the interests of their employees at heart, as many managers claim they do, they've done a bad job of convincing their employees of this fact.

The problem is obviously one of misunderstanding, born of poor or insincere communications. Management, through this entire era of growing crisis, has maintained a stoic silence about itself. Meanwhile, its detractors have hacked away at it, weakening its very foundations, and management has said nothing. It's getting awfully late!

Managers must take some positive steps to bridge the awesome empathy gap that currently exists between themselves and the people they employ. Let's consider some of the things that management could do to improve its image and simultaneously help itself regain its right to manage.

Labor-Management Negotiations

A typical collective bargaining session can be historically compared to the seal show at a three-ring circus. Back in the early days of labor-management negotiations the scenario consisted of management assuming the role of the ringmaster, with labor representatives playing the part of the trained seals. The act consisted of the ringmaster barking several times, after which the seals would bark back. With these preliminaries out of the way the ringmaster would then throw the seals a fish. After a half century of these theatrics the analogy is still valid. There has been one minor change: in today's collective bargaining session it is labor that plays the role of the ringmaster.

This role reversal did not come about through Darwin's theory of evolution. It occurred because management permitted it to occur. Throughout the years management has continued to operate on a policy it formulated back in the early days of labor-management negotiations when concessions were made unilaterally by management simply because management was the only group that had anything to give.

This concept is, of course, no longer valid. Yet management, for the most part, has failed to wake up and smell the coffee. It has convinced both the union and the employees that it is a ruthless tight-fisted entity that can be induced to make concessions only by tremendous pressure exerted by financially well-heeled groups. It's admittedly a little late for management in organized shops to exclude unions from the industrial scene. I'm not sure this would even be beneficial. Nevertheless, management must get the message across that gains in pay and fringe benefits must be geared to corresponding gains in productivity. Both workers and the unions that represent them must be made to realize that the best way to improve their lot under our current economic system is to produce more goods and services rather than periodically intimidating industry with blue-sky demands.

Lest I be accused at this point of being a union-busting radical, permit me to interject that, over the years, I have enjoyed an extremely good relationship with union officials in numerous industries even though I was initially retained by management. The rapport I have developed with labor unions serving a dozen or more industries has been acquired through the simple expedient of mutual respect. My files contain numerous letters of commendation from union officials at the national level stating how we were able to secure increased benefits for their membership through improved operational procedures that were subsequently shared with the workers. I have specifically been named in several union contracts as an arbitrating agent. In my experience, unions will usually listen to reason if management's thinking is valid and presented in good faith with a genuine concern for the worker's welfare.

I recall an incident that occurred a few years ago at a parts assembly plant in the Midwest where we were called in after the company had been encountering severe financial setbacks. An investigation of the company's history showed that the firm had originated in the founder's basement, but it had grown to a status of six plants and 375 employees with $6 million in annual sales. This growth had been achieved through a policy of quality production, close management vigilance over costs, and piecework rates high enough to offer a real incentive to workers yet low enough to be sound and economical.

Then came a period when changes such as increased competition and new technology began to slacken management's grip. Shortly afterward a union stepped in and pressured for changes in the piecework rate structure. Within months the entire piecework pattern swerved off course. Costs began to surge, productivity slackened, and the company began wallowing in the pool of red ink. Matching the union's pressure for bigger pay boosts was the sales department's demand for an end to price increases. The ultimate result was that quality control fell apart, work methods degenerated, and the work flow deteriorated into a state of utter confusion.

A comprehensive study revealed the fact that for the company to remain solvent it would be necessary, among other things, to discard the present piecework system and install a standard hourly incentive plan geared to obtaining a fair day's production for a day's pay, commensurate with other companies in the same industry.

Management accepted this proposal readily but the union was adamant in its demand for retention of the status quo. To cope with this we worked up, with the assistance of company management, a presentation designed to give graphic evidence to union officials that if the employees gave full cooperation, wage levels could be maintained and might even be increased. It was made clear through presentation of irrefutable facts and figures that the alternate choice, rejection of the program, would endanger the company's very existence and the existence of the workers' jobs.

It was then explained that the proposal, which included job evaluation, foreman training, work scheduling, work-flow changes, and work simplification, would be implemented with the assistance of union officials and key employees, who would be free to make proposals and suggestions relative to the program's development.

After some minor modification the proposal was accepted by the union and subsequently agreed to in a vote by the union's membership. To assist in selling the program to the workers we took the trouble to draft a comprehensive letter, which was sent to each employee, that outlined in detail the aims and benefits that would be acquired by the modified procedure.

The story has a happy ending. The initial projected company savings of $100,000 annually actually turned out to be a conservative estimate. Labor costs were reduced by 12%. Average take-home pay for employees was actually increased. And the company is now operating on the black side of the ledger. Moreover, I have it on the word of company management that since the program has been placed into effect there has been a remarkably improved spirit of cooperation between management and union officials.

This program succeeded, in my opinion, because primarily both the union and the employees were not only made aware of the need for changes, but were given a hand in the program's implementation. The pity is that the company almost went into bankruptcy before the parties involved faced up to the true facts and took appropriate corrective action. This story is very representative and could be duplicated in many organizations.

Who can honestly blame the unions for taking advantage of a free lunch that they must neither buy nor help to cook? It's also hard to blame workers for holding the false belief that the union represents a benevolent god who can secure things for them that they'd have trouble getting by themselves. Management has permitted this state of affairs to evolve. To change this condition, management must develop a new attitude and a set of collective bargaining ground rules that both the unions and the workers accept. It must do this soon. Management has already given away most of the store while scarcely considering the cost of its inventory investment.

Here are a few suggestions designed to help management live with the union shop and still retain its right to manage.

How to Live with the Union Shop

Prepare for labor hearings or collective bargaining sessions as you would for a court case or an IRS audit. Management, for the most part, fails to do this. Get rid of any ideas you might have that organized labor is a semiliterate group of radicals that can be conned by a few superficial promises. Nothing could be further from the truth.

Leaders of the labor movement have been taught by experts who know all the right formulas and are not afraid to apply them. Recognize this and act accordingly. Regard the union as an equal, but only as an equal. Organized labor now has enough goodies that negotiations can be conducted on a give-and-take basis instead of on the tacit understanding that management *always* has to give something away without getting anything in return.

Conversely, never go into a labor hearing or bargaining session with a chip on your shoulder. Managers can no longer afford to feel they have the right to set all the rules simply because they happen to own the football. Management must wake up and consider the cost of the erroneous idea that it knows it all and doesn't have to be prepared to meet with labor. Each time management meets labor with a patronizing attitude, each time it treats labor negotiators as a bunch of poorly equipped schoolboys instead of the well-prepared, well-informed leaders they are, management leaves itself open to lose still another round of a contest in which, traditionally, management has come out second-best.

If plans are being developed for changes like building a new plant, making a change in the management structure, buying another company, closing a plant or division for a while, or expanding a department, tell your employees about it. *And tell them first.* Management is privy to policy changes before anyone else. Isn't it a bit ridiculous to get scooped on this type of information by the labor press?

Programs involving employee participation should never be implemented without first selling the supervisory group on the change. This applies to job evaluation plans, time and motion studies, merit rating, or any other programs affecting employee take-home pay or fringe benefits. Better still, assign the foremen a role in developing these plans. We all like to be told in advance. Therefore, once you've sold a plan or policy to supervision, spend a little additional time selling it to your workers. Giving them advance information will enable them to see and appreciate the advantages instead of just the shortcomings that may be exaggerated through the rumor mill.

I feel strongly enough about this that in the course of several presentations I have made to management groups I've taken the trouble to prepare a prescription bottle containing three capsules. I distribute these items to each of the members of the audience with the explanation, "This medicine, if used properly, can cure most of your management's ills. Since I am not a physician the capsules do not, needless to say, contain any drugs or conventional healing powers. Instead, inside each of the three capsules is a small piece of paper containing a single piece of advice. The three comments are as follows:

1. Information breeds understanding.
2. We all want to be told in advance.
3. We will all cooperate in a program in the same proportion that we are part of that program."

Selling Your Workers

American management is supposed to be the best in the world when it comes to selling its products, but it has done a miserable job of selling itself to the American worker. If your workers are forced to depend on the union, the grapevine, or rumors at the corner beer joint for their information, your present program simply isn't accomplishing its purpose. Management must do something about its problem of convincing employees that it cares about their welfare.

When was the last time you took a hard look at your employee evaluation program? How does it operate? Is it a vital part of the administrative policy or is it simply considered a necessary evil by the people responsible for its overall function? A well-run job evaluation program gives management much more than an insight into individual performance. It is a morale improvement factor and it can bring to light facts to talk about during labor negotiations.

Does your company have a workable policy for promotion from within? Do your workers believe in it? Has any clear-cut policy been established so that workers may improve their status within the organization? This is one area where management is not usually in competition with the union, since it is to the union's advantage *not* to lose its membership to the ranks of management.

Are wages, benefits, and other personnel policies and practices in line with the industry and the area? Have any studies been made about this? If not, why not? Is your company interested in community affairs? Is the community interested in your company? This is an important factor if you are required to draw on local labor supply. An occasional press release to your local newspaper concerning company affairs and events can do wonders for your company image.

Many managers tend to forget that the most valuable commodity in their organization is the people who make it function. It's surprising how a little idea such as letting employees select from three color schemes for a plant or office can perk up morale. A simple voting measure adds to the pride employees have in the place where they work and at the same time makes them feel a little more important.

An effective device to assure better employee communications is to check with employees regularly to determine their current feelings toward the company. Employees should be surveyed at least every three years to determine their complaints and attitudes. When trouble spots are noted as a result of the survey, they should be corrected. And once corrections have been made it is important to report back to the workers and advise them of the action taken. Between these official surveys, ways should be devised to sample employee opinions and reactions on a day-to-day basis.

In any labor-management communications program, care should be taken to avoid trying to cram free enterprise down the employees' throats. Most of them are tired of hearing about free enterprise. They just want to live in it. Tailor your communications program to report all the news, but don't overglorify the company. Let's face it, no one is more familiar with the shortcomings of an organization than the people who work there. Any attempt to distort facts or manage the news will immediately be obvious and further detract from management's credibility.

Some years ago I had the privilege of being included in the Japanese Productivity Conference, an honor I hastily accepted in the light of the vast productivity strides that have been accomplished by our Far East trade partners. One of the most interesting findings at these sessions was the fact that Japanese workers are consistently more dedicated to their jobs than their American counterparts. It is common practice, for example, for a Japanese worker who is entitled to three weeks of vacation to turn back one week as a show of good faith toward the employers and fellow workers.

In return for this, Japanese management evidences a remarkable goodwill toward the people who produce its goods and services, contrary to the image some people hold on the subject. Barring extremely adverse conditions, a Japanese worker is assured of a job with the company for life. Pay during sick periods, including pregnancy, goes on regardless of length of illness. Monotonous and repetitive job functions are, if possible, replaced by automation, and the people displaced are transferred with appropriate training into more creative and interesting work. Unions exist but often work hand in hand with management and sit in on management meetings, where they contribute valuable input conducive to greater job satisfaction and productivity.

In the light of the labor-management climate in America, any current attempt to transplant all of these policies to a Detroit auto factory would be doomed to failure. Yet there is no doubt that the empathy that normally exists between labor and management in Japan is a king-sized factor in the glaring difference between the two countries in productivity and balance-of-trade figures.

Perhaps, in view of how far labor has progressed in America, it is impractical to suggest that American workers would even consider an arrangement of this type. Changes of this scope are, admittedly, difficult to bring about. However, if our industrial leaders were unilaterally to develop a program designed to convince their employees that they truly have their interests at heart, those leaders might be surprised at the reciprocal benefits they would acquire in return.

The Company Newsletter—Benefit or Farce?

One of the most effective devices for improving labor-management relations is an employee-circulated newsletter. It can reap huge benefits in employee goodwill *providing* it is developed and prepared in a manner designed to appeal to the real interests of the workers who constitute the readership. Sadly enough, however, most company publications not only fail to improve communications, they often have an adverse effect on management-employee relations.

Ask a dozen rank-and-file employees what they think of their company's newsletter and there's a good chance most of them will freely admit they seldom bother to read it. Further questioning, particularly if done by someone outside company management, will probably produce replies like "brain-wash," "propaganda," or simply "uninteresting reading." In view of the almost universal indictment of what should be one of management's most effective tools, it seems appropriate that the people who publish or formulate the policy for these publications take a hard look at what they're doing wrong and decide what, if anything, can be done to correct the unfavorable image they have created.

A primary source of reader dissatisfaction is that company-issued publications have been permitted to deteriorate into one-sided instruments that publicize only the interests of the company and management's side of any given issue. Employees have been conditioned to expect some degree of responsible journalism in a country that claims to maintain freedom of the press. After being fed a steady diet of management-controlled news over a long period of time, they strike back, either by refusing to read the offered material or by attempting to discredit it.

If you doubt that management is either being overselective or just plain "copping out" in the handling of in-house material, take a look at a typical issue of a company newsletter and then compare it with a similar publication put out by the company's union. Look at the type of material offered by the union newspaper: real down-to-earth gutsy stuff like economic facts, what union members are getting—or are going to get. By contrast, the front page of a company publication may offer a profile of the second vice president in charge of sales, whose accomplishments or family history couldn't matter less to a bench hand working in the tool room. It interests me that in over 30 years of association with top management I have yet to see a union publication in an executive office.

More often than not the wishy-washy reporting in company newspapers stems from the fact that their editors, or employees responsible for selection of material, are operating under a severe handicap. As administrative or semiadministrative employees, editors feel that they should represent management's point of view. Yet, paradoxically, they are also charged with the responsibility of communicating with labor, which comprises the top-heavy majority of the readership. The result, unless the person responsible for the newsletter's contents is either an extreme extrovert or unusually talented in the field of written communication, is usually a lopsided version of the news, heavily weighted in favor of management.

Also, the responsibility for the newspaper's contents is too often entrusted to some barely qualified member of the office staff who just happens to have the available time to muddle through the admittedly time-consuming duties with a minimum degree of effectiveness. The obvious solution is, of course, to select competent personnel to handle the program and give them the license to cover topics that are meaningful to the people who make up its readership.

Another basic fault with company publications is that they tend to fall into the habit of being issued on an irregular basis. I know of one company that issues a newsletter only when it is faced with some type of labor crisis. It is then trotted out to express management's views. Since this occurs only when the going gets rough or when the labor press is snapping at corporate fetlocks, the action fools no one, and is actually so obvious that the publication is a standing joke among employees, who laughingly refer to it as "The Management Brainwash."

If a newsletter is worth publishing, it's worth publishing on a regular basis. By getting people into the habit of expecting it you create a condition where they will find themselves looking forward to reading what it says. This is good. If employees are informed by an official source, they don't have to settle for the distorted version of the news acquired through the company grapevine.

In the preparation and editing, care should be taken not to overglorify the company. I know of a firm that operates an extremely well-run nonunion shop. Employee benefits are good and compare favorably with most union shops in the same industry. Possibly because of this, the company has thus far managed to survive attempts by the union to organize the plant. The president of this firm is an extremely capable and knowledgeable man. He has but one serious hangup—an irrational fear of his organization's becoming organized. Since this man is also the company newsletter's editor and chief contributor, each issue contains some exaggerated and completely distorted version of the merits of his firm as a place to work. It also contains several thinly veiled references to the dire consequences that will befall his workers should they make the mistake of voting in a union shop.

At the moment a majority of the personnel still favor a nonunion operation, but the vote gets closer each time the union makes a bid. Should the union move in, its victory will, in my opinion, have been caused primarily by the completely unrealistic propaganda this man is attempting to cram down the throats of his workers, all of whom are intelligent enough to recognize the obvious intent of his distorted editorializing.

Most company newsletters fail to answer the questions that are foremost in the minds of employees. Numerous subjects make effective copy and will generate improved labor-management relations. Subjects like condition of the business, outlook for the future, price situations, labor situations, wage situations, shortages, competition, legislation as it affects the business, new customers, and policy changes are all meaty material that if handled honestly will be faithfully read and even enjoyed by the workforce.

Additional subjects are employee benefits, tax information, new orders, quality control, statistics, and, of course, personnel news—providing it is not top-heavy with management-oriented material. Pages of pictures of the company president at ribbon-cutting ceremonies become wearisome and are often construed (sometimes rightly so) as attempts by the editorial staff to butter up the top brass. Since nonsupervisory readers probably outnumber management readers by a ratio of at least ten to one, the basic slant should be toward the worker. If an article is included that applies only to management, it should not be put in top lead position. This is an *employee* newsletter. If you want to print something for management, do it separately and circulate it exclusively among managers. If the company is large enough, you may wish to consider a separate supervisor's newsletter mailed to the foremen's homes on a confidential basis. You might be surprised at the goodwill that can be acquired by this simple communication device.

Finally, don't ignore unsavory conditions that you know about. Face up to unpleasant facts, meet them head on, and take a position. Your readers may not always agree with your stand, but they'll appreciate your forthright presentation and honest approach. The important thing is to be sincere and present the facts, basing judgments on conditions as they exist at the time the newsletter goes to press. If it turns out you're wrong, you can change your position later. Oddly enough, even a correction of a previous statement can sometimes enhance your image in the eyes of your employees.

It takes a brave person to stand squarely up to the issues and consistently tell it like it is. But if you print a newsletter, like it or not, you're in the publishing business. And telling it like it is is what publishing is all about.

There is no substitute for sincerity in the world of communication. It is the yardstick by which the people in management and its programs are measured. When management speaks up with sincerity its voice will be heard.

The Ten Commandments of Good Communication

Following is a summarizing set of guidelines to be used in conjunction with an employee relations improvement program. I call it the Ten Commandments of Good Communication, and it has proved so successful that it has been used as a basic guideline for many successful programs.

1. *Be sincere. You can't make red out of blue.* Modern communication between employer and employee has, in a dangerous number of instances, consisted of pure propaganda for the employer. In these instances the communicators have overlooked the fact that their job is to build goodwill and understanding. Instead they try to spread a favorable smokescreen around the organization. Communication must be honest and sincere to be successful. Otherwise, it may enjoy acceptance for a time, but inevitably em-

ployees will look with mistrust upon management statements.

2. *Be simple and unaffected in your language.* Whether it's oral or printed communication, be conversational. Many management messages are stuffy and uninteresting. Talking to employees involves a conversation, not a commencement address.

3. *Don't overglorify the company.* Harsh as it may sound to the sentimentalists, the plant is a place of brick and mortar and glass. It's full of people with good habits and bad habits, with pleasing dispositions and disagreeable personalities. If it's a normal organization, it has had triumphs, disappointments, labor serenity, and labor strife. To attempt to paint it as an industrial Eden is an insult to your worker's intelligence.

4. *Select competent personnel to handle the communications program.* A successful communications program requires people of many practical talents, including meeting employees and getting along with them, writing simply and sensibly, knowing what constitutes a story and how to put it together, and great tact combined with sincerity of purpose.

5. *Make communications a top-level management responsibility.* If a communications program is to be effective, it must have the blessing, encouragement, and cooperation of the front office. The industrial editor or communications director working ten notches down on the industrial totem pole, with no access to the policy-making level, is as ineffective as a wax spark plug. If the program is to reflect top management thinking, the person who is to interpret that thinking must be directly exposed to it. Chief executives simply cannot afford to evade the issue with the weak argument that they're too busy to give personal attention to anything as vital as the people who produce their goods or services.

6. *Don't ignore unsavory situations your employees know to exist.* If your program is to have acceptance, be realistic. If you have labor trouble, talk about it. If the plant has been struck, say so. If you have unpleasant situations that your own people are discussing, have the courage to discuss them sincerely and openly. Employees hear enough double-talk

from our nation's politicians without being subjected to it on the job.

7. *Investigate all devices of communication and use them.* There are numerous communication devices. Some are made to order for the large company. Others work more effectively in a small operation. The individual or group meeting with employees, involving personal contact, is the best of all. And the best single channel of communications is through the first-line supervisor. Never exclude the foreman from your communications program.

8. *Check constantly on the effectiveness of your program.* The investment you make in a communications program should show results. They may be less tangible than the results of an advertising drive but they can be measured. Surveys of employee opinion have become more sensible and scientific. Employees, if properly approached, will appraise communications devices frankly and sincerely.

9. *Never let your communications program slow down.* The good program is a continuing device. It's a day-in, day-out effort to provide a continuing stream of information to employees and to encourage a flow of employee reaction and opinion in return.

10. *Finally, meet the people.* There are no swamis in industry good enough to read the minds of people they don't know. Any communications experts who think they can mastermind a continuous program from behind a desk are kidding themselves. Communications, by definition, must be a two-way street.

ten

Probing Productivity Problems in Other Areas

Take away our factories, take away our trade, our avenues of transportaton, our money. Leave us nothing but our organization, and in four years we shall have reestablished ourselves.

Andrew Carnegie

Given today's business climate, one might wonder if Mr. Carnegie, faced with our current problems, could have been this optimistic. There appear to be forces at work during these closing years of the twentieth century that seem intent on stifling all efforts to improve productivity. What is even more frightening is that all the efforts of our advanced technology seem unable to cope with the situation.

Why did an acceptable rate of productivity improvement exist in an earlier era and then disappear when man's achievements have literally exploded into space? This question has so many facets that it is doubtful if anyone will ever come up with an explanation that is satisfactory to all concerned.

The fact remains that the situation does exist. I happen to believe that it has been caused largely by the factors described so far in this book, but additional segments in modern industry are also ailing and in great need of some vigorous therapy. Some of them are cited in this chapter, together with suggestions for improvements.

Taming the Paper Tiger

So much has been written about the need to improve paperwork procedures that I often wonder whether the paper used to publish all this information does not exceed the paper savings derived from publication of this material. Nonetheless, a few decades ago the paperwork requirements for a small company could be neatly (or not so neatly) contained in the pigeonholes of a roll-top desk. Today the same operation will probably require several file cabinets and a couple of full-time office clerks. Larger operators have been forced to add anywhere from five to fifty additional employees simply to cope with assorted forms, invoices, carbon copies, and other miscellaneous scraps of paper.

This paperwork explosion has been brought about by a variety of reasons. Cost control and analysis have, to a large degree, replaced country bookkeeping. Data processing has a voracious appetite for fresh paper. Xerox machines are often overworked simply because they exist. Government regulations gobble up a vast array of forms and reports.

Can this paperwork monster be eliminated? Probably not. Contrary to much publicity by AT&T to persuade the public to conduct business by telephone (much of which is in the form of the printed word), paperwork, if properly used, is a valuable administrative tool. It provides written evidence, it establishes responsibility for issuing an order, it eliminates duplication of instructions, and it generates goodwill.

Nevertheless, *excessive* paperwork is a factor that cuts deeply into the operating costs of a majority of today's organizations. Fortunately, there are ways by which this paper tiger can be controlled, even if it cannot be eliminated entirely.

The most effective method for doing this is a sweeping and comprehensive program designed to challenge the need for each type of communication currently being used. The program should start with the company's file cabinets. Every file cabinet in the office, when full, represents several thousand dollars' worth of clerical effort. Add to this the initial cost of equipment, floor space that could be used to better advantage, and time wasted by people who have to review copies of forms and memoranda that serve little practical purpose and the staggering cost of this paperwork begins to come sharply into focus.

In challenging the need for the items contained in file cabinets it is well to be guided by a few basic questions. (1) How important is the information, really? (2) Is it duplicated elsewhere? (3) What would happen if we didn't have it? Answer these questions honestly and very often you'll find that file storage areas can literally be cut in half.

Another costly practice is the age-old system of supplying each branch or section with a copy of everything that might remotely concern its operation. This is a throwback to the old army system where military protocol demanded that every portion in the chain of command be advised of the movements of each unit. It has no place in modern business and should be eliminated except where the need for it is completely obvious.

The use (rather, abuse) of unnecessary forms is another area where huge savings can be accomplished. Too often we find that forms are poorly prepared, serve little useful purpose, or because of changed conditions contain information that is ineffective or could be secured elsewhere. Unnecessary forms can often be eliminated by an analysis of all the forms used by an organization, asking the following questions: (1) Is the information needed? (2) Is another source available? (3) Does the cost of obtaining the information exceed its worth? In conducting this analysis often you'll find that two or three forms can be combined in a manner that actually increases their efficiency because it helps to tell the complete story.

Still another area for improvement in paperwork procedures is the interoffice memo. Savings of a significant nature can be acquired by streamlining procedures used for interoffice communications. This can be done simply by conducting a survey based on these questions and followed by appropriate corrective action.

1. Does everyone to whom this correspondence is directed understand it?
2. Can the number of people to whom correspondence is routed be reduced?
3. Can check boxes be used to reduce the amount of routing information?
4. Can office symbols be used for routing?
5. Will the use of colored paper help in the distribution of these items?
6. Are all memos of a standard size for convenient filing?
7. Is the memo's subject clearly stated in the upper-right-hand corner for quick location in the files?
8. Can a window envelope be used?
9. Can self-mailers be used?

Designing a Better Suggestions Program

Whether it consists of a wooden box next to the time clock that is emptied periodically, or a full-scale program requiring the services of several employees, a suggestions program can be a valuable device that if properly designed and monitored will result in important cost savings with an added incentive bonus to workers who are close enough to an operation to observe areas where improvement might be indicated. Unfortunately, the suggestions system as it is employed today is often expensive to operate and frequently results in a lowering of morale on the part of employees who must, of necessity, face rejection of ideas that were submitted in good faith.

The greatest single threat to any suggestions program is the lack of a positive attitude on the part of the people who analyze and evaluate the suggestions. If a suggestions system is to work, management must refrain from taking the all-too-familiar attitude that if an idea were any good, someone would have already thought of it. Admittedly, not all suggestions can be implemented. A report compiled by the National Assocation of Suggestion Systems states that only 25% of the suggestions offered in a given year are subsequently accepted. In most cases the rejection is warranted. Often disapproval is based on factors that were unknown to the suggester. In many instances the cost of implementation would exceed the benefits derived. Nevertheless, in numerous instances valuable suggestions are summarily dismissed because of snap judgments and arbitrary decisions.

The importance of getting several evaluations prior to passing judgment on a suggestion cannot be emphasized too strongly. The most effective way to do this, and one that is *not* employed by the majority of today's organizations, is the chain-of-command approach in which the initial evaluation is performed by the employee's immediate supervisor, after which the file is passed up the administrative ladder until it reaches someone with authority either to implement or to conclusively reject the proposal. Under this method suggestions approved and implemented at a low management level are subsequently forwarded directly to the Suggestion Awards Committee, thus significantly diminishing the not inconsiderable amount of paper shuffling that usually accompanies a program of this type.

It could be argued that under this method top management runs the risk of losing control. However, the huge paperwork savings, combined with the additional and badly needed prestige for lower-level managers, will more than offset the risk of an occasional bad decision. Furthermore, the problem can be partially overcome by placing a member of top management on the Suggestion Awards Committee,

or by having work orders pertaining to suggestions chan-
neled through a member of top management.

An extremely sensitive area in any suggestions program
is what to do about proposals that must be rejected. This
often requires considerable tact—especially in borderline
cases where some benefits are obvious but the cost of placing
the idea into effect would be prohibitive. A verbal rejection,
unless the person chosen for this detail is extremely skilled in
employee relations, may often do more harm than good and
can frequently deteriorate into a bitter dispute. To take the
sting out of rejection a personal letter (*not a form letter!*) will
usually result in a minimum of resentment, particularly if the
door is left open for some recourse in the event that a mistake has been made, or that later events cause a change in
thinking on the subject.

Another area where controversy occurs is in the amount
of money to be awarded for adopted suggestions. Many businesses award 10% of the first year's savings to the suggester.
However, suggestions concerning issues like safety and training involve intangible benefits, so some additional yardstick
must be devised. A minimum award of, say, $20 with an
upward scale for unusually beneficial proposals would appear to be reasonable in instances of this type.

Like all other facets of modern business a suggestions
program must contain two basic ingredients. The first is a
reasonable return to the company for the money it invests
for implementation. The second is a fair compensation to the
people who contribute their time and effort to making the
enterprise work.

Selling Productivity to the Sales Division

Programs designed to cut costs, develop better standards,
increase work output, or reduce inefficiency have become a
standard practice in American business. Methods employed
to accomplish these measures include stopwatch techniques,
complex charts, expensive consultants, and even computer

analysis that can be programmed to almost every area of a company's operation.

Nearly all these plans are directed primarily against operations, which includes direct and sometimes indirect labor. This is ironic because operations is an area that even in normal times is under continual scrutiny from supervision at all levels. Almost always overlooked is the fact that the sales division, which is the direct key to higher earnings, has more often than not been permitted to operate with a minimum degree of guidance and with few attempts to initiate any system of checks and balances.

The premise that a sales division can best operate under a hands-off policy is often rationalized by the argument that the salesperson is closer to the customers than anyone else and is therefore better able to determine their needs and degree of receptiveness to a company's products. Another argument for a hands-off policy is that a salesperson's income is contingent upon sales and therefore salespeople will take it upon themselves to do whatever is necessary to move a maximum amount of the company's products.

With all due respect to the American salespeople—most of whom are competent, knowledgeable, and receptive to fresh ideas—the premise that salespeople operate best without any guidelines or restraint is as invalid as the flat-earth theory! Salespeople, while admittedly interested in making sales, are also human and therefore in need of (and often desperately desirous of) some comprehensive guidelines, or at the very least an overall operating policy that is geared to sales. Considerable evidence shows that top management in many industries has failed to provide this necessary ingredient.

Management in these companies is going to have to face up to the indisputable fact that the sales force is an important facet of the operation. It can literally make or break an organization. Therefore, it should at the very least be subject to the same rules of management operation and control as the people who operate a lathe or an office typewriter.

Granted, the art of selling requires considerable subtlety

and tact and is not the sort of thing that can normally be resolved by a canned list of do's and don'ts. Nevertheless, observations made at a number of different companies have turned up a surprising number of recurring weaknesses, either in the sales operation or in the manner by which top management is directing that operation. Here are some illustrations of these areas of difficulty, together with suggested remedial action.

1. *Salespeople are often allowed to sell what they want rather than what the company directs them to sell.* This is basically a management problem and stems from lack of communication between the sales force and top management. Frequently salespeople are treated as subordinates by top management and sales managers. Seldom are they advised on a company's internal problems or the profit structure on various products. Consequently, they often go into the field with only a vague knowledge of exactly what is expected of them.

The problem will probably not be resolved by half measures or by the company president delivering a superficial pep talk at the next sales meeting. What is needed is a better sales staff–management relationship, followed by a comprehensive training program for salespeople in which it is clearly outlined exactly what the company wishes to accomplish, what it hopes to sell, and what its priorities, its capabilities, and its shortcomings are. This action should then be backed up by a complete reevaluation of sales incentives based on a graduated scale of percentages that are proportionate to the lines that management most hopes to sell.

2. *Salespeople often concentrate on the big order and give only perfunctory attention to other prospects that, with a little attention, could develop into a sizable source of additional revenue.* In some cases this policy has even been endorsed by managers who either issue instructions not to take on small accounts, or, as happens more frequently, give tacit approval when salespeople turn up their noses at small orders.

There is probably no greater practical illustration of the futility of putting all one's eggs in the same basket than a competitive operation like selling. Despite this, many salespeople, and in some cases their employers, appear content to sit smugly on a few large accounts, complacent in the knowledge that repeat orders will continue to roll in with the same regularity as the monthly telephone bill.

One of the most distressing facts of life for the business person is that a continual influx of *new* business is necessary to offset the attrition of gross revenue caused by lost accounts. This is an elementary law of business survival.

3. *Most companies fail to reapportion sales efforts in a manner designed to motivate the sales staff to sell on a basis of equipment utilization.* It is an unusual company that does not possess at least one piece of equipment that is idle to a degree where it fails to justify the floor space it occupies and the maintenance required to keep it in working order. Yet, oddly enough, seldom is any meaningful effort made to secure enough additional work to keep this equipment in operation. Again, this is not the fault of the sales division. It is a top management problem. The solution lies in providing the salespeople with a sound working knowledge of the organization that pays their salaries and then developing incentives for sales personnel designed to make greater use of equipment that might otherwise be idle.

4. *Many salespeople lack a comprehensive knowledge of the entire industry as opposed to the product they are trying to sell.* With a better background in the needs of the industry and the manner in which it operates, salespeople are in a better position to anticipate the needs of the customers as well as talk to them about their own problems and how to resolve them. One means of creating this ideal situation is, of course, to hire salespeople who have a background in the industry in which they are trying to sell. Since this is not always possible or practical, the best alternative is to include in the sales training curriculum at least some general information about the industry.

Too many management people lose sight of the fact that the people with whom a salesperson must associate are quite knowledgeable about the industry that provides them with their bread and butter. These people might be much more receptive to doing business with someone who has at least taken the trouble to learn the difference between a parapet and a parakeet.

5. *Too many salespeople are paid on gross sales rather than on percentage of profit to the company.* It is one of the basic laws of economics that everyone loves a bargain. Accordingly, the customer who is looking for a bargain can be expected to direct more attention to items on which the company makes a relatively small margin of profit. The problem is further complicated by the fact that a salesperson who is paid on gross sales can be expected to push the items that are easiest to sell.

The solution is a commission structure based on percentage of profit to the company. There's no denying that this involves some work, presents some problems, and requires more bookkeeping than a policy based on gross sales. Nevertheless, the modified procedure can pay huge dividends for a company and is usually welcomed by the more competent sales personnel for the obvious reason that they can make more money.

6. *Sales managers often lack the qualifications to provide meaningful leadership to the sales force they are supposed to direct.* In many instances sales managers appear content to function in a figurehead status, with little or no thought of developing guidelines or providing operating policy for the department they are supposed to oversee. Another frequent complaint is that many sales managers forget the necessity of getting into the field often enough to know problems firsthand. Because of this they may develop a distorted viewpoint, based on second- or thirdhand information. Many of today's sales managers achieved their present status because they originally were top salespeople. This is fine if they possess the qualities of leadership necessary for the job. However, the criteria for a good sales manager and a good salesperson have no more similarity than the criteria for a high-production worker and a good foreman. In either case, if the company promotes a person solely on the basis of performance on the old job, it may find that it has lost a good producer and gained a poor supervisor.

7. *Salespeople, because of the competitive nature of their occupation, tend to work primarily for themselves rather than for the company.* This characteristic extends, at times, to withholding information and techniques that would be helpful to other salespeople working for the same company. The practice is particularly prevalent when a firm generates sales competition through the use of contests and other gimmicks designed to pit one salesperson against another.

A degree of information sharing can often be achieved by requesting each salesperson to make a brief presentation before the entire sales group and in the presence of top management. At this meeting each salesperson is asked to describe what type of sales technique has been particularly successful in his or her case.

The knowledge that they are presenting this information to top management, as well as to their peers, will, more often than not, motivate salespeople to come up with their *best* pitch—if for no other reason than to make a better presentation to top management.

8. *Many salespeople are burdened with excess paperwork.* During periods of economic crisis, most companies cut overhead in the front office, and in the process they often load the resultant paperwork on the sales force.

When we consider the comparative value to the company of a first-rate office clerk and a first-rate salesperson, it becomes clear that if a salesperson is losing effective selling time by performing credit checks or some similar type of office chore, he or she is not operating at maximum effectiveness. Add to this the fact that many salespeople are not really qualified for this type of work and it becomes painfully obvious that the company is indirectly paying a price all out of proportion to what the job is really worth.

Generally speaking, salespeople should be required to do only two things as far as paperwork is concerned: call reports and expense reports.

9. *Salespeople make too many promises that can't be kept.* This is a problem that is extremely prevalent and falls squarely on the shoulders of the sales division manager. Unlike the sale of sand from a bottomless pit, the sale of most manufactured

products is contingent upon availability of equipment and skilled manpower. In spite of this, many salespeople promise services that cannot be provided and set deadlines that cannot be kept. True, some jobs are complex and might conceivably be difficult to estimate. Nevertheless, when a company fails for the third or fourth time to provide services contracted in good faith, the customer can be expected to react with something short of complete impassiveness.

The solution to this problem is so obvious that it is one of the mysteries of life why the problem occurs so often. Salespeople who have not learned enough about the physical layout of a plant to make an intelligent estimate should contact someone in operations before setting dates, rather than making any promises that are based on sheer guesswork.

10. *Management often fails to keep the sales force informed.* This is another of the many problems that must be shared jointly between top management and the sales division. Good salespeople often make a conscious effort to keep up with changes that occur within the industry in general and their own company in particular. Yet all too often management, by failing to recognize the sales force as an important part of the operation, invites situations in which salespeople are unaware of factors that are obvious to everyone else from the company president to the night watchman.

The solution, of course, lies in improved communications concerning things like business outlook for the future, price situations, policy changes, new customers, new competition, and a variety of other topics that should be called to the attention of the sales force on a regular basis.

Salespeople, because of their conversational abilities, often give the impression of being extroverts. Nevertheless, they have feelings too, and morale problems. By keeping them informed you'll convince them you have their interest at heart and perhaps improve the total operation in the process.

The items noted above are all *recurring* problems and comprise only the most obvious areas of difficulty that exist between management and the sales force that sells its product. From these observations, and stated in the most charitable manner possible, it must be concluded that a huge empathy gap presently exists between the people who produce the product and those who sell the merchandise. In most of the cases noted above, the solutions are better communications between operations and sales, and a sales division that is exposed to the same management rules as the rest of the corporate structure.

As the pressures of the economy increase we will probably be forced into some of the remedies pointed out in the previous pages. It is high time we recognized the sales division as neither an untouchable nor one of industry's stepchildren, but rather as an important function of the business structure that is subject to the same rules observed by coworkers in operations.

The Case for Quality Control

"The appalling lack of quality control in America is a serious contributing factor to our declining rate of productivity." When I made this statement to a business associate recently, he countered with the statement: "It might be a factor, yet in the strict sense of the word, quality control tends to somewhat inhibit productivity by taking workers who might be productively employed and reassigning them to nonproductive duties and additional paper shuffling." This attitude is, unfortunately, shared by many of today's industrialists.

It may brand me as something of a maverick, but I must strongly disagree with the premise that quality control does not pay for its own manpower expenditures! Those of us who grew up in the 1930s can vividly recall the Japanese products that filled the counters of our nation's department stores. They consisted of watches that didn't work; wind-up toys that ceased to function the day after Christmas; and papier-mâché knicknacks that were given away at the local movie houses on bingo nights. The commodities imported from Japan in those days were cheaper than their American counterparts, yet the law-mandated inscription "Made in Japan" was all that was required to generate a huge "buy

American" movement despite the worst economic depression in our history. The notion of Japanese inferiority in the field of manufacturing was slow to die, even after Japan began racking up huge productivity gains while American factories were struggling to barely balance productivity improvement with increased operating costs.

"Sure they're producing more," was the consumer attitude, "but look at the quality of the merchandise. American products are constructed better. So they're worth a little more." You don't hear much of this kind of talk any more, except perhaps on some of the TV automobile commercials. And if there are those among us who are being persuaded by this type of Madison Avenue oratory, few of us are carrying our convictions to the Big 3's automotive showrooms.

In 1980 Japanese car makers turned out 11 million cars and trucks—2 million more than were manufactured by Detroit. These vehicles are a far cry from the worthless junk that was synonomous with the Japanese products of another era. They are, for the most part, well built, gas-efficient, and constructed under standards of quality control that are virtually unheard of on American assembly lines.

Toyota maintains a quality control system so efficient that defects appear in less than 1% of the newly completed cars that roll off the line. Much of this is attributable to automation that far surpasses United States standards. In 1979 Toyota produced 50 cars per production employee—five times the American average! In the meantime 300,000—36%!—of America's auto workers are unemployed, all American car manufacturers are losing money, and perhaps the less said about Chrysler Corporation the better.

The auto industry is, of course, only one segment of the industrial scene where Japan and other countries have made deep inroads into America's share of the market. Makers of TV sets, musical instruments, motorcycles, and other products too numerous to mention no longer hide the "Made in Japan" label on an inconspicuous area of their products, but openly and proudly advertise the origin of manufacture in full-page magazine displays and spot TV commercials. When they can be persuaded to emerge from behind their corporation's public-relations smoke screen, many American industrialists reluctantly agree that American-made products are generally more prone to defects than their overseas counterparts. When approached about building factories in the United States to take some of our unemployed auto workers off the unemployment rolls, Japanese car makers bluntly state they're afraid to build factories in America because they fear the quality of our labor.

The apathy of American industrialists toward strong quality control measures seems to be based on the premise that quality control can be lumped together with operations like safety, environmental impact regulations, and other government-controlled indirect labor factors that must be absorbed as part of the cost of doing business. And since quality control is the least-regulated factor it is also the first to fall under the ax of cost-cutting measures.

This is short-sighted reasoning. A vigorous program of quality control will return benefits far in excess of the man-hours required to implement the procedure. Quality control, or lack of it, affects productivity in the following ways.

1. Complaints about product defects must be processed. This requires additional administrative man-hours and time spent in complaint investigation.
2. Defective products still under warranty must be replaced at company expense.
3. Minor problems that could be corrected as they occur become major problems if left unchecked.
4. Customer dissatisfaction results in fewer sales and a lower share of the market.

Since there seems little room for doubt that we have been outmaneuvered in both quality control and productivity by foreign countries, particularly Japan, it seems appropriate that we consider not only what *we* are doing wrong, but what *they* are doing right.

The threadbare argument that Japanese workers receive less pay than their American counterparts simply doesn't wash any more. In 1980 salaried workers in Japan earned an average of $25,700 per year, and the average annual income of all Japanese employees was about $17,000. Ninety-one percent of Japan's 116 million people now freely admit that they belong to the middle class and can boast of having all the niceties in life that are commensurate with this status.

What brought all this about? The sharp rise in productivity and quality control is almost universally credited to a period in history shortly after World War II when Dr. W. Edwards Deming, an American mathematical physicist, was invited to Japan to teach statistical methods to Japanese industry. It is important to bear in mind that the image of Japanese consumer goods at the time was at the lowest point in history. Yet Dr. Deming, by working together with a renowned quality control specialist and with Tokyo University professor Dr. Kaoru Ishikawa, developed a national program that is credited with reversing the scarred image of Japanese-made products and changing them into sought-after commodities throughout the world.

The nucleus of the plan devised by Dr. Deming and his associates centered around the introduction of a management system of statistical techniques, including control charts, process capabilities, and statistical sampling plans, augmented by quality control circles. A quality control circle (or QC circle) is a small group, usually not exceeding 10 employees who do similar work, that voluntarily meets once a week for the purpose of discussing problems related to quality. At these meetings solutions are recommended and, when possible, implemented. The groups are all taught elementary techniques of problem solving, including statistical methods. Typical problems include reducing such things as defects, scrap, rework, and machine downtime.

In 1978 there were about 88,000 registered QC circles in Japan, consisting of 700,000 members. Estimates of both registered and unregistered QC membership put the total figure at about 8 million workers. The quality control principle might seem somewhat overly simplistic until one analyzes the complete ramifications of the process and takes into consideration the Japanese work attitude. The viewpoint of a Japanese worker toward his or her job can best be described as one of complete and utter dedication. To remain idle when there is work to be done is a trait seldom observed in Japanese industry. A worker's job in Japan is regarded as something that will provide the worker with the good things in life and should therefore be nurtured with reciprocal care and devotion. The simple act of talking about activities unrelated to the job during working hours is considered to be in extremely bad taste by the Japanese worker.

Japanese managers, to a greater degree than their American counterparts, recognize their workers as an integral part of the organizational structure. They go to considerable lengths, both on and off the job, to make employees feel more secure. Participation of all personnel in both job-related and free-time activities is common practice in Japan, with the company sponsoring many family social events. Employees are virtually never discharged from an organization, except under the most unusual circumstances.

The end result of this policy seems to be that Japanese management has succeeded in convincing the worker that he or she will be taken care of at all times without resorting to strikes, grievance procedures, unemployment insurance, and the dozens of other regulatory practices so common in the American industrial complex. The system has worked extremely well in Japan, possibly because the Japanese attitude toward labor-management relations is about 180 degrees removed from the thinking in American industry. Yet even if we concede that importing the Japanese work attitude wholesale to an American factory is impossible, there have been numerous instances where the QC circle and its related methods have worked well in America.

One case involves Westinghouse, where the QC program is called "Volunteers Interested in Perfection" (VIPS). A similar program at Boeing titled "Participative Employee Problem Solving" (PEPS) has been enormously successful. A bolder approach has been successfully used at the Grand Rapids, Michigan, plant of the Japanese-owned Yamaha Mu-

sical Products Inc. Productivity at this plant, predictably perhaps, had fallen far below that of its sister plants located in
Japan. Management (which is about half American and half
Japanese) therefore sent some of its American employees to
Japan for a one- to three-month training period. There they
were exposed to the customs and traditions of their position
by Japanese standards and acquired a better understanding
of the Japanese industrial scene. Upon returning to their
jobs in Grand Rapids they were enrolled in a vigorous program of discussion among plant workers designed to create
an atmosphere of greater cooperation between labor and
management. Since the Yamaha program was first initiated,
productivity at the Grand Rapids plant has risen dramatically.

These are, of course, relatively isolated instances. The
principles of statistical controls for quality augmented by QC
circles, introduced by Dr. Deming over 30 years ago, have
been slow to catch on in America. In an interview with the
editors of *Quality* magazine and published in the February
and March 1979 issues, Dr. Deming pointed out that the
principles he brought to Japan in 1948 received little attention in America. "They were well received by engineers," he
said, "but management paid no attention to them."

Concerning the future outlook for quality control in
America, Dr. Deming is similarly unencouraging. He be-
lieves that the QC gap between Japan and the United States
will widen even further in the years ahead. "Americans depend too much on inspection," he says. "And inspection is
unsatisfactory. Even 100% inspection using automatic testing
machines doesn't guarantee quality. It's too late—the quality
is already there." What's needed, according to Dr. Deming,
"is a nationwide commitment to quality. The Japanese made
that commitment nearly 30 years ago and are still learning
and moving ahead faster and faster."

All this adds up to the fact that we don't have to learn
anything about the principles of quality control from Japan.
We invented them. All we have to do now is apply this knowledge. Let's hope that we'll begin to do this before we're hurt
too badly to recover.

Organization Is More than Just a Beautiful Chart

I have seen many beautifully drawn organization charts. Some of these were incredibly complex. Some were in living color. Some of them even contained three-by-five photos of the incumbents to the indicated position. Yet I have never seen an organization chart that ever told me anything.

Organization charts, for the most part, provide an interesting decoration on the wall of the chief executive's office, and little more. Let me hasten to explain that these remarks are directed at organization charts and not organization, which is a vital and necessary part of any well-run business. Unfortunately, however, many company executives refuse to differentiate between the two. Instead they regard the organization chart as something akin to a sacred proclamation upon which the firm's entire operational structure must be based for all time to come.

Any organization chart, even one that is accurate and well maintained as far as company personnel is concerned, is essentially a static thing. It represents the chain of command in a company at a given point in time. An organization, on the other hand, is anything but static. It changes pattern day by day, week by week, in response to events, improvements, and business climate. The changes in an organization are brought about by human behavior. Whether or not this human behavior takes the form of a weak general foreman or a lawmaker who cares little about the firm's general interest is unimportant as far as the chart is concerned. Charts do not reflect these changes. They simply hang majestically on the wall, usually unchanged in structure, with company management serene in the belief that The Organization Chart is the final and ultimate design for the company's operating road map.

The almost universal worship of the organization chart did not come about through mass telepathy between the managers of our nation's leading firms. The practice has been ingrained through many years of management education that attempts to scientifically design an organization structure that would fit any and all business. I submit that this is a throwback to the sales pitch given by the snake-oil salesmen of another era, who peddled medicine that was supposed to cure all diseases from leprosy to trench mouth.

Because they are influenced primarily by human factors, good principles of organization cannot be brought about scientifically. Yet many management textbooks have attempted to do this. Graicunas's theory outlines a formula that tells exactly how many people should report to any particular manager. According to Mr. Graicunas, no more than five or six people should report to any one person, yet many well-run companies have far more reporting to key executives.

People, together with their capabilities and shortcomings, must always take priority over the bloodless requirements of an organization chart. The relationships should be based on the jobs, the people in the jobs, and the conditions surrounding the jobs. Otherwise we are sacrificing results for rituals.

I know of one case, for example, where it made sense for the chief industrial engineer to report to the controller because the manufacturing vice president was heavily sales-oriented and the works manager was wrapped up in product research. On the other hand, the controller was deeply interested in the management implications of industrial engineering. Principles of organization are admittedly necessary, but they should be kept flexible enough to fit existing conditions. Additional problems concerning organizational responsibilities are often caused by overlapping lines of authority and poorly prepared job descriptions.

In designing job descriptions, particularly for managerial and semisupervisory employees, the best advice is to keep the definitions as broad as possible if they must be made at all. The catch-all phrase "and such other duties as the installation head may prescribe" has, I know, been overworked. On rare occasions it might even be abused. However, when compared with the abuses that have occurred because of superspecialization, the damage has been negligible.

If we are ready to accept the premise that good organization must be geared to the people in the job rather than the job itself, the logical question follows: How can a clear and workable standard of performance be developed? The initial step is to prepare the ground for definite responsibility for which management can hold accountable the entire executive or supervisory group. In general, executives understand their main responsibilities, especially if they have written job descriptions.

As an example of an effective way to proceed, let's take the sales manager. His or her primary responsibility is to produce more sales and thereby improve the profit position. From a realistic standpoint it is debatable whether we can hold sales managers responsible for *total* sales, since they do not control things like the weather, changes in buying habits of customers, or quality of service provided by individual plants. They can, however, be held directly responsible for improvement of the selling organization, for concentration of effort by all sales personnel along proper channels, and for obtaining specific performance. They can also be held accountable for total sales budget performance and, to some extent, sales stability.

To arrive at a standard, the president, controller, and individual executives should jointly determine the acceptable range of performance for each standard that will apply. The available data on that standard in terms of industry performance, company performance, and individual performance should also be considered, as well as the influence of differing ranges of performance on a given standard upon sales and profits. With these data, it should not be difficult for everyone concerned to arrive at an agreement on what is necessary in order to accomplish the results that the company expects in terms of total sales or profitability.

Once standard performance has been attained for one or more positions—and geared to the individuals in the position—the entire organization can be developed into a more workable unit based on individual responsibility and accountability and knit together by clearly delineated lines of authority. The method of accomplishment will vary somewhat depending upon the company itself and the people who make it operate. However, here are some principles I have found effective as general guidelines for better organization. I've never seen these rules in any textbooks. They have been developed during long years of experience.

1. There should be a policy or "road map" set up before the organization is formed or a reorganization contemplated.

2. There must be a yardstick for measuring accountability.

3. Because there are no scientific rules of human behavior, a scientific approach to the problems of organization will create more problems than solutions.

4. To have employees in certain positions report to a predetermined officer of the company is ridiculous. Workers should report to the *logical* person, to be determined by the job or other conditions. There should be no cut-and-dried rule about who is to report to whom—it all depends on the setup or specific conditions within the company.

5. Organization and its tool the organization chart are only means to an end, not ends in themselves.

6. Top management must realize that any organization is in a continual state of flux. It is subject to change every time personnel or production policies or sales methods are changed.

7. Sound management practice recognizes that any person in an organization can be replaced. Ideally, the chief executive should be able to look at the organization and ask: "Could I fire that employee tomorrow if it were necessary?" If the answer is no, management could be in for big trouble.

8. Good organization cannot exist without 100% participation.

9. There is a definite relationship between the size of the company and the necessity for formalized organization.

10. To bring about good organization, one should forget theoretical ideals and accept the fact that personnel is the keynote: the employees that are available, or can be made available, to the firm.

Once true organization is achieved, an organization chart might then be in order. If one is drawn up it might be

helpful to prepare it according to the same general principles used by the men who drafted our Constitution. In other
words, recognize that it is designed to operate only at this
point in time, and as changes occur amendments may be
necessary. Otherwise, the charts rather than company management could end up running the organization.

Summary

Since this book opened with the analogy of labor, management, and government as the legs that support a three-legged stool representing industry, it is perhaps fitting that we close on a similar note.

I have tried to present the industrial situation today as I see it and share some of the methods by which I have solved many commonplace problems. Both government and labor (two of the legs on the allegorical stool) have been subjected to some strong, and I believe well-earned, criticism. I have, however, been particularly harsh on management, with full realization that most of the people who read this book will be managers. Many of them have probably bristled at some of the uncomplimentary things I've said about practices that may now be standard procedures in their factories and offices.

As I stated in the preface, if you are only mildly disturbed by the things I have said, I am disappointed. Frankly, I hoped to get you so worked up that you would go back to your company and do something about the productivity gap that now poses such a serious threat to our entire economic system. To those readers who may feel that I have spent a disproportionate amount of wordage on the management segment of our economy, permit me to explain why I sincerely believe that management must assume the greatest portion of the blame.

First, I believe it's important to recognize the fact that both government and labor, no matter how sympathetic toward solving the productivity problem, are both motivated by interests that, if not downright selfish, are at the least personal bread-and-butter issues. Managers, on the other hand, are *being paid* to make sure that the productivity level of their company will be high enough to bring the firm a reasonable return on its investment. But even more importantly, few would deny that of the three entities, management is in a vastly better position to initiate remedial action against the numerous shortcomings cited in this book.

If we agree that both government and labor have been apathetic if not downright hostile toward productivity improvement, the logical question follows: What has management been doing while the ship is sinking? And unfortunately the response of managers, for the most part, has not been overwhelmingly reassuring.

A poll conducted by Louis Harris a few years back pointed up the fact that nearly half of all executives agree with the widespread premise of organized labor that productivity gains benefit companies at the expense of their workers and that productivity gains are usually contingent on workers being displaced by machines or on employees working much harder. Therefore, with neither side fully committed, productivity improvement can best be compared to a painful therapy for a serious disease that both doctor and patient refuse to fully recognize.

Incredibly enough, there even seems to be some confusion concerning exactly what is meant by "productivity." Without worrying about other people's definitions, I'd like to submit my own simple, logical definition of productivity as it applies to today's industry: the ratio between what is produced and what must be consumed in order to produce it.

Regardless of semantics, the bottom line appears to be that since neither government nor labor is willing to take any giant steps toward remedying our productivity deficiency, this leaves one, and only one, area in our economy that is equipped to run the ball on this very important issue—*management!*

Management must get enthusiastic and serious concerning the subject of productivity improvement. It must act, not talk! Reversing the present trend won't be easy. It would be helpful if government and labor would cooperate with the king-sized effort that will be required to bring this about. Yet before this can happen management must take the lead. Otherwise all we can hope for is more unrealistic demands by organized labor and more campaign oratory delivered by our nation's politicians in meaningless generalities because specifics concerning productivity improvement might offend a portion of the voting public who might be asked to work a little harder.

I'd like to believe that America is up to the challenge we face in the years ahead. History clearly indicates that we, as a people, have the ability to overcome almost any adversity once we clearly recognize the need to do so. In my lifetime I have seen our country recover and prosper after the worst depression in history. When our naval fleet was shattered at Pearl Harbor, we possessed the will, the dedication, and the fortitude not only to rebuild our devastated war machine, but also to ultimately achieve unconditional victory.

While the nations of Europe were sifting through the rubble created by that giant conflict, I watched American money, equipment, know-how, and ingenuity combine to restore and rebuild the crumbled cities both of our allies and of the defeated countries. Through the magic of television and space technology I have marveled at a close-up look at Saturn's rings and watched men walk on the moon. If all this sounds like flag-waving I accept the indictment proudly. This country has been good to me. Yet all the things that I currently enjoy were acquired by a system of productive enterprise that now seems to be slowly slipping away.

Our democratic lifestyle has given us the highest standard of living that the world has ever known. There are few among us who do not cherish our democracy. However, because it is a democracy, we cannot function as many of our authoritarian neighbors do. We cannot *legislate* changes in our approach to increasing our national productivity. We cannot even bring these about—

Unless . . . our federal government gets really interested in doing the job that should be done for the good of the country instead of what is good in terms of winning votes. It must work objectively and cooperatively with both management and labor.

Unless . . . organized labor realizes that continued increases in wages and fringe benefits for its members can come only from increases in productivity. Union leaders must recognize this and convince their membership of the validity of this concept.

Unless . . . both labor and management agree on common goals. Such agreement, incidentally, has been a key factor in Japan's skyrocketing productivity.

Unless . . . managers realize that they have an obligation not only to their stockholders, but to consumers, their employees, and the entire country as well.

Without these actions the three-legged stool is in grave danger of collapsing under its own weight. For our own sake, and that of everyone in this nation, we cannot permit this to happen.

Index